THE LIBRARIAN'S FACILITY MANAGEMENT HANDBOOK

Carmine J. Trotta

and

Marcia Trotta

Neal-Schuman Publishers, Inc.

New York   London

Published by Neal Schuman Publishers, Inc.
100 Varick Street
New York, NY 10013

The paper used in this publication meets the minimum requirements of American National Standard for Information Sciences—Permanence of Paper for Printed Library materials, ANSI Z39.48–1992.

ISBN 1–55570–400–X

Printed and bound in the United States of America.

Library of Congress Cataloging-in-Publication Data

Trotta, Carmine J.
    The librarian's facility management handbook / Carmine J. Trotta, Marcia Trotta.
        p. cm.
    Includes index.
    ISBN 1–55570–400–X (alk. paper)
    1. Library buildings—Maintenance and repair—Handbooks, manuals, etc.
    2. Library administration—Handbooks, manuals, etc. I. Trotta, Marcia.
    II. Title.

Z679 .T76 2001
022—dc21   00–059290

For Christopher

Table of Contents

List of Figures

Preface

Overseeing the maintenance and repair of a library's building, heating and cooling systems, plumbing, and other aspects of the physical plant is perhaps the most intimidating part of a library director's job. Library school curricula don't include these topics and most members of the profession may not be particularly adroit when it comes to the ins and outs of either fire protection systems or roof repair.

Facilities maintenance is often complex, occasionally overwhelming, and always a never-ending responsibility. Before assuming a position that brings with it partial or total responsibility for building maintenance and repair, it's difficult to imagine what the management of a facility actually entails. As you worked your way up the ladder to your present position did you consider what being "in charge" actually meant? I'm sure you assumed that as a facilities manager you would have people around to assist—janitors, contracted workers, and maintenance crews. If you manage a large library or a library system, you no doubt have many of these people to turn to for advice (and actual work). The great majority of libraries, however, are quite small and the librarians who manage those facilities don't have this kind of help and assistance. Even if a library is cleaned under a contract by a cleaning firm, the library director is usually responsible for keeping the building in good repair, noticing if the roof leaks, getting the broken air conditioning fixed, and planning for long-range physical improvements. *The Librarian's Facility Management Handbook* is designed to identify, organize, and help you create a plan for carrying out the diverse array of responsibilities entailed in this critical aspect of your job as a library administrator.

Specifically, this book is designed to:

- outline the basic responsibilities reasonably expected of you as an administrator, so you can make sure the buildings you oversee function properly
- provide a framework that will guide you in assessing your facility to determine the strengths and the weaknesses existing in your library building and establish a baseline against which you can measure your progress
- recommend simple, straightforward methods for solving maintenance problems
- help you design, implement, monitor, and evaluate an effective development and maintenance plan for your facility, so you get the maximum value

for the dollars your organization invests in its buildings, while increasing the efficiency of the operation

As an administrator of a library, you should take great care to be up to date on equipment, technology, trends, and issues that concern the world of libraries. The time has come for us to move beyond simply calling in the "expert" to do a repair and then authorizing payment. The administrator needs to exhibit strong leadership in orchestrating what needs to be done on a regular basis to keep the facility viable, functioning, and attractive. We believe it is essential that the administrator acquire an in-depth knowledge of how and when facility operations and upgrades for these operations should take place. It is important that the administrator be able to look at the situations at hand from the perspective of contractors that may need to be hired, as well as from his own. There is no doubt we want to do as good a job in taking care of our building as we do in overseeing all of the other responsibilities that go along with the library's operations. Knowledge and planning are keys to success.

Purpose

For any organization, but especially for organizations that are part of a government or nonprofit entity, the facility is often a primary asset as well as the workplace that produces our "product"—quality service. Facilities management is more than a plan to keep our buildings in good repair. It is a system to strategically control the costs involved in directly supporting the organization's mission and productivity. Libraries are much more than a storage place for books and materials; patrons use our buildings for meeting space, for study space, and as activities centers. The everyday wear-and-tear on these facilities is significant, and our job as administrator does include keeping the facility safe and effective for all of its uses, while simultaneously controlling costs.

Increasingly, the administrative areas of the nonprofit world are gravitating toward the sound business practices of the corporate world. Clearly, we would not imagine major corporations ignoring the systems that house and support the activities that cause their businesses to flourish and make a profit. Why, then, would any nonprofit do otherwise, even though our objectives and our "bottom line" are different? No matter what the mission, the workplace must support the particular functions expected to happen there. It must take into consideration staff movement, common traffic patterns, and technological impacts, as well as the work that must be done. After all, what we hope to achieve is to make the environment of the library seamlessly support each aspect of its mission. The result will offer better service and satisfaction to a very diverse public.

Audience and Scope

The Librarian's Facility Management Handbook is intended for any librarian who manages a library of any type or size. Even if the librarian is not the person who will actually do the hands-on work at or in the facility, she is often the one who must supervise the person who does the maintenance.

We created the book to be as useful to someone new to the job, with little or no experience in facilities management, as it is to veteran managers interested in improving and updating their facilities management plans or looking for new ideas that work. Even the most experienced library administrators agree that facilities management is more complex and difficult than it was even a few years ago. The infrastructure required to support today's information technology tops the list of things that make maintaining a facility today more difficult. In addition, many of us have inherited an aging building that not only needs to be retrofitted for today's technology, but also requires repair and replacement of basic building systems. *The Librarian's Facility Management Handbook* was written with these two major issues in mind.

While we do not intend to supply a blueprint for every situation, we have tried to provide a comprehensive overview of most situations you will need to plan for as a successful facilities manager. This handbook was also designed to help you cope with the "day-to-day disasters" that require you to make operational decisions quickly. This guide's many checklists will assist you in these situations. There is no question that, with budgets that are often restrictive, it is tempting to ignore a loose ceiling tile or the drip of a faucet. Perhaps, we have even gone so far as to think, "If I close my eyes, this leak will go away." We have all learned firsthand how small problems ignored will escalate into larger, more expensive problems when they are not handled properly. *The Librarian's Facility Management Handbook* provides an ongoing, preventive maintenance program helpful in avoiding these pitfalls and preventing some of the more serious building problems that could occur. Being prepared and having the knowledge necessary to cope with these situations is by far safer than waiting for a crisis to occur and learning to deal with it in "the trenches" through trial and error.

How to Use This Book

We designed *The Librarian's Facility Management Handbook* so you might approach the information in a manner to suit your needs. We recommend reading cover to cover to gain the most comprehensive understanding of the material. Of course, we recognize the need to find pertinent, useful instructions as quickly as possible, so we formatted the text as a real handbook. Each of the nine chapters begins with a numbered overview of the key points. These separate points follow with illustrative figures of samples, examples, and checklists supporting the subject.

We begin *The Librarian's Facility Management Handbook* with various aspects of day-to-day operations typical in a library.

Chapter 1, "Maintaining the Daily Operations," shows you how to develop and staff an effective maintenance management policy, oversee personnel and custodial staff, manage maintenance contract work, establish housekeeping space and standards, and assess your maintenance program.

Chapter 2, "Supplying Utilities and Energy Management," addresses all areas of electrical service, air conditioning and ventilation, water supply and maintenance, plumbing, boiler maintenance, heating systems, and energy audits. Here we examine telecommunications, including phone options, Internet Service Providers, and Digital Subscriber Lines.

Chapter 3, "Providing the Right Environment," examines the issues both inside and outside of the library. Inside, we report on lighting, air and water quality, and humidity issues. Outside, we explore the grounds by considerating standards; how to best care for lawns, shrubs, and trees; practical pest control; and Occupational Safety and Health Administration guidelines (OSHA).

Then we move on to the bigger context of facilities management.

Chapter 4, "Budgeting and Controlling Costs," discusses the finances of facilities management, organization for budget preparation, purchasing power, grants, proposals, project bid information, and insurance issues.

Chapter 5, "Keeping Records and Managing Reports," looks at the importance of a central recordkeeping system. It includes preventive maintenance programs and how to determine the priority of maintenance work, inspections, inventories, record retention, bids and purchasing procedures, contractor's liability insurance, work requests, and equipment repair.

Chapter 6, "Designing Safety and Security Guidelines," offers strategies to effectively deal with emergencies, assemble a comprehensive safety plan, establish safety committees, defuse difficult situations, conduct video surveillance, and tackle insurance issues.

Chapter 7, "Preparing Emergency and Disaster Plans," considers fire drills, fire alarm systems, emergency communications, hazardous areas, incident reports, and treating injuries.

Chapter 8, "Arranging Space and Considerations for Special Needs Patrons," shows you how to make the most of space, implement adaptive reuse, address the needs of people with special needs, and adapt low cost solutions for reasonable accommodation. It includes extensive suggestions, samples, and checklists from the Adults with Disabilities Act (ADA).

Chapter 9, "Complete Guide to Supplies, Services, and Resources," presents a great deal of helpful information on supplies, equipment, and tools; recommended supplies to keep on hand; supply sources; services; building regulations; reference material; and recommended Web sites.

The final section is a glossary of essential facilities management terms.

We, the authors, wrote this volume based on our "real" experiences. Marcia Trotta is a library director who often turns to coauthor Carmine Trotta, a professional facilities manager, for direction and advice on various issues concerning the library building. We believe it is important that you find someone you can trust and to whom you can turn for advice if you do not feel you have the background to make a facilities decision. We have written this volume with the hope that it will become one of the sources upon which you will come to trust and depend.

Acknowledgment

A very special thanks to our editor, Virginia Mathews, for her patience in assisting us with this volume. Her thoughtful comments made us take a close look at the information we wanted to include so it would be most helpful to librarians everywhere.

1 Maintaining the Daily Operations

Overview

Figures

1.1   Overview of Day-to-Day Operations

To take care of a facility is to preserve the building so it can function for the purpose intended. Establishing the policies and procedures that are related to a building management program is a crucial function performed primarily by the administrator, with duties assigned to designated individuals who are charged to assist with this program. It is fundamental that any program be designed so the administrator can ensure the building will function in a manner that is supportive of the functions of the library. In addition, the administrator must be knowledgeable of the basic principles of facilities management, including safety and sanitation, building repair and renovation, as well as beautification issues.

1.2 Developing a Maintenance Management Policy and Action Plan

Establishing a plan for building upkeep is not different from any other strategic planning process. The administrator must decide exactly what it is that a facilities management plan will accomplish. The purpose of the program should be clearly outlined; goals and objectives should be written in a detailed fashion. They will then provide the specifics that will be accomplished through a variety of tasks.

As with other planning activities, it is important that the staff be involved in the plan's development if it is going to support everyday workplace functions. The plan must encompass common usage, as well as technical and workflow patterns, so the functions of the library will be accommodated and staff will be able to get their job done. Good communication among the administration, front-line staff, and the individuals who will be implementing the plan on a day-to-day basis is important for its success.

If thoughtfully developed, a well-written maintenance management policy can be the driving force behind a successful maintenance department. In a practical policy, daily action plans are outlined. Although these will differ somewhat from library to library, the essence of the policy is to define what needs to be done in order to provide maintenance services that will allow the library to carry out its functions. The facility must be maintained at a level that is consistent with the required quality and quantity of work or service that is to be delivered.

A maintenance plan should describe what is expected of staff at all levels of the organization and there should be general guidelines for achievement. While it is not expected that the staff of the children's library vacuum their carpets every day, it may be expected that, if there is a spill during a craft program, they clean up after themselves. This type of action may be required before damage becomes harder to repair or dirt is ground into the carpet and is more difficult to clean.

As with any policy, the tone and substance of the maintenance policy revert to the mission statement of the library system. The maintenance department, then, defines its mission within the scope of the entire library organization. Finally, the goals are outlined and supported with a series of action steps that will be taken to accomplish them. Following such a process will ensure that the library has an effective maintenance management system in place with all the aspects covered.

It is important that all staff know and understand the schedule that the maintenance staff will follow on a regular basis. This is so staff can inform the maintenance crew if what they have scheduled will interfere with a library offering. It is also a good idea to have a "chain of command" so that individual staff members don't give conflicting instructions to the maintenance crew. People with maintenance responsibilities need to have a clear understanding of how their tasks fit with others in the overall plan and in what time frame they are to be accomplished. However, maintenance personnel should follow the orders of their immediate supervisor, not of every library employee.

The maintenance plan must clearly make provisions for what is to be done, when and how, and by whom. It is the director's responsibility to make sure the expectations for particular jobs are clearly defined. In large systems, the director may designate another administrator or the facilities manager to convey these expectations. Appropriate feedback to and from staff about the work done, and the amount of time that it took, will be useful in establishing future expectations for given situations.

The library director also has the responsibility to make sure the maintenance program does not conflict with the operations of the facility. A written policy can help avoid this problem. As an example, you would not want to have the maintenance department schedule the resurfacing of the parking lot during National Library Week, when the programming department has a full schedule of activities, and there will be no places to park!

The following is an example of a maintenance program plan that can be adapted to suit the needs of your particular situation. Further detail will be provided later in this chapter to illustrate how the plan becomes action.

Figure 1–1
Maintenance Program Plan

Mission:

The purpose of the Main Street Library's maintenance program is to increase the life of the building and its systems, to ensure the safety of the occupants and of the equipment, to ensure sanitary conditions for both users and staff; and to maintain an attractive appearance, while ensuring that the service priorities of the library are protected.

Goals:

1. to operate the library in the most cost-effective manner

2. to ensure the reliability of the building systems and compliance with health, safety, and building codes

3. to provide housekeeping or cleaning services to maintain the facility to the established standard

4. to respond promptly to repair any malfunctioning systems

5. to establish a preventive maintenance checklist to prevent failure of equipment or structures

6. to maintain accurate records of equipment repair, operations manuals, utility usage, and so on

7. to seek ways of reducing total operating costs while maintaining acceptable standards of maintenance for daily operations

Objectives:

1. to clean the facility on a daily basis according to established priorities

2. to evaluate competitive vendors for all building maintenance supplies

3. to perform periodic preventive procedures to extend the life of equipment and structure

4. to establish an approved list of vendors who can be expected to respond to system failures

5. to update building information files on a weekly basis

As in any plan, goals are long-range and objectives are short-term activities. The following is an example of detail that can help clarify what must be taken into consideration over a period of time.

Figure 1–2
Almanac for a Year-Round Repair and Improvement Schedule

January:	Indoor work
	Heavy cleaning
	Patching, painting walls
February:	Inspection of fire and security systems
March:	Inspection of plumbing and water supply
	Inspection of electrical system
April:	Indoor remodeling
	Shampooing Rugs
May:	Exterior work: roof, gutters, downspouts, chimney flashing
	Air conditioning start-up
June:	Masonry work, painting, residing
July:	Window repairs
August:	Resurfacing driveways and parking lots
	Cleaning or changing filters in heaters and boilers
September:	Installation of weather stripping
	Caulking, winterizing
October:	Garage door repairs
	Chimney repairs
	Rustproofing
November:	Cleaning leaves, gutters
	Outdoor pipe repairs
December:	Waxing floors
	Polishing and repairing furniture

This is a calendar that gives a broad picture of the work that needs to be done every year. We planned it seasonally. You may want to adjust it to fit your particular climate and locality.

1.3   Staffing the Maintenance Program

While the administrator has the overall responsibility for the maintenance of the facility, he is usually not the person who completes the tasks, although we know many library directors who have mopped a floor or vacuumed a carpet when needed! Realistically, the administrator has to plan and continue to be thoroughly familiar with the schedule of maintenance in order to know if the job is getting done properly. In some libraries, daily oversight may be delegated to an administrative assistant.

Some libraries have staff on the payroll who fulfill the tasks that need to be accomplished for the maintenance program. Other libraries may contract out with a service that does the housekeeping and cleaning tasks. While, at first, this may seem to be more cost effective than having people on staff, and being responsible for their benefits as well as their salary, it is not always the most cost-effective solution. Someone at the library (and it often ends up being the director) still has to inspect the various aspects of the facility to make sure they are in good repair. Someone will need to determine if there are problems and who to call for help. Neglected or postponed maintenance can eventually lead to serious problems. There may be a need to replace elements of building or equipment rather than repair them, and you might then have a budgetary crisis on your hands. Therefore, we suggest that you weigh your options carefully before determining which course of action to take.

Figure 1–3
Defining the Responsibilities of the Facilities Manager

Every library will want to designate someone as the facilities manager. In large libraries, a staff position may fit this description. In others, it may be the library director or a person who is designated to fill the duties. In any case, it is an important function. The extent of her responsibilities will be dependent on the particular circumstances at a particular location, but the following can be used as a guide to what is expected. The facilities manager

- originates work orders

- oversees ongoing housekeeping

- oversees the maintenance and repair plan

- authorizes expenditures

- with the director (or in the director's absence), is the library's command person in emergency situations

- has authority to shut down if there are unsafe conditions

- is responsible for the quality and the quantity of supplies and equipment purchased

- is able to accept or reject orders

- schedules, conducts, and facilitates inspections and energy audits

- is the library's liaison with contractors and vendors

- keeps baseline information about the facility in an organized schedule (see Chapter 5)

- establishes both long-range and short-range plans for the facility

- assists the director with operational and capital budget projections

1.4   Janitorial and Custodial Employees

Janitorial and custodial maintenance workers perform housekeeping services for the organization. This support function not only involves a clean and orderly place in which to work, but also has a definite role in management's responsibility to provide a healthy and safe work environment.

One of the main responsibilities that falls to the facilities manager or the director is the evaluation and assessment of either the employees who have this janitorial responsibility or an outside cleaning service that has been contracted with. In order to do this successfully, it is important that there is a standard on which to rate completion of tasks. The job description and a list of regularly assigned duties may be useful for this process and provide a fair benchmark against which to measure satisfactory performance.

The job description can also be used as the basis of writing a contract with an outside service. If at all possible, we recommend that the work be done while the library is closed so it does not interfere with patrons. If staff report before opening to the public, this might be the best time for the cleaning service to be there, so that adequate supervision can be provided.

Figure 1–4
Custodian or Janitor Job Description Samples

Here are two sample job descriptions that cover the scope of work that can be expected from custodial staff. These examples may need editing in order to comply with particular local situations.

Custodian Job Description I

Purpose: The custodian will be responsible for cleaning and maintaining the library and will be able to perform minor repairs.

Examples of Work: Duties may include, but are not limited to: cleaning of all areas of the library, including sweeping, vacuuming, dusting, and polishing; disinfecting rest rooms; replenishing supplies; clearing sidewalks of debris, leaves, snow, and ice; replacing lights; setting up and taking down chairs; minor repairs, preventive maintenance, and reporting the need of further repair to the library director.

Skills, Abilities: Custodians should have a knowledge of cleaning methods, materials, and equipment. They should also be knowledgeable about safety practices. Custodians may be required to bend, stoop, and reach; lift up to 50 pounds; adhere to schedules; follow basic instructions; and work independently in the absence of a supervisor.

Education and Experience: A high school diploma is recommended. Basic ability to learn cleaning practices is required. One year of general custodial experience is desirable.

Custodian Job Description II

Job Function: Clean and maintain orderly conditions throughout the library.

Representative Products, Materials, Processes: Cleaning floors, walks, walls, fixtures, furniture, exhibit cases, and so on. Sweeping, mopping, scrubbing, shoveling, polishing, buffing, washing, waxing, wiping, dusting. Materials: water, cleaners, soaps, detergents, wax, polish, disinfectant, de-icer, and so on.

Tools to Be Used: General-use janitorial tools and equipment such as brooms, mops, snow shovels, street brooms, pails, wringers, sponges, dusters, and vacuum cleaners; polishing, shampooing, and buffing machines.

Major Duties: Perform general cleaning operations. Empty waste receptacles and sand urns into collection bins. Clean floors by sweeping, dusting, damp mopping, shampooing, buffing. Perform other janitorial duties such as dusting window sills and moldings; cleaning stairs and glass door panels; vacuuming and removing spots from carpeting; cleaning and disinfecting drinking fountains; washing soiled areas of doors, walls, and furniture. Other duties include cleaning restrooms: washing and disinfecting basin and toilet fixtures; cleaning and filling soap, paper, and other dispensing equipment. Remove snow from walkways; sand as needed. Prepare lists of needed janitorial supplies for management. Perform other duties as assigned.

1.5   Oversight of Personnel

Sometimes management assumes that since custodial work is relatively low skilled, little planning or training is required. This is not so. In order for a library's maintenance program to be effective, planning and training must be precise and thorough. A clear and carefully developed custodial plan can reduce both overall maintenance costs and inconvenience. This list of goals and objectives, or tasks, will work in conjunction with the overall maintenance plan for the facility.

In order to determine what these tasks are and the priority in which they should be accomplished, we recommend that you follow the following process.

First, determine what type of custodial care will be necessary to keep your facility in good condition. Walk through each of the areas of the library and list what types of items and spaces must be cared for on a periodic basis. It is important to remember that the use of library space changes over time. The observer should note the number and placement of chairs, waste baskets, and other movable items. This is useful information that is needed to plan a work schedule.

Next, estimate the amount of time it should take to do each task under ideal conditions. Once this is complete, the facilities manager will be able to develop cleaning methods and times. Look at each area to determine the sequence and the methods of cleaning, and establish priorities for the frequency of cleaning particular areas. Take into account ceilings, light fixtures, furniture, stairs, aisles, wastebaskets, floors, windows, and window coverings in all parts of the building. Then determine the frequency with which each item is cleaned, the method that is to be used to clean it, and what supplies and equipment will be required to do the job correctly.

The facilities manager will then have a clearer picture of the number of in-house staff needed to carry the workload or will be able to share this information with an outside vendor if a cleaning contract is to be awarded. In either scenario, this preliminary assessment will be the basis of determining the cost of custodial services as well as giving clear directions to the people who will be performing the tasks. If necessary, show those who are to do the tasks the methods of performing them so they will meet the library director's expectations.

The facilities manager or the library director will periodically need to perform quality checks to see that tasks are being completed. This is a way of evaluating the custodial staff or the cleaning service to determine if the plan is effective. As with any type of evaluation system, it is crucial that problems be corrected. The use of a checking system will allow the supervisor to determine if there are tasks being done that are not necessary or if there are other ways of accomplishing the intended action that could potentially save time and money. Feedback to custodial staff is just as important as it is with any staff member.

Telling staff that they have done a good job or advising of some areas that need to be improved is part of the overall management role. The same is true when using an outside company.

Instead of having custodial and maintenance staff, some libraries contract out these needed services to a private vendor or provider. In some cases, this becomes more cost effective because the benefits package for employees is then picked up by the outside company. However, there are other issues that develop when an outside provider is selected. These include quality of work, supervision of the provider, evaluation of the provider, and security issues related to the provider being in the building when library staff is not.

A word should be said about the relationship the library director needs to have with an outside company. It is important that the director have the name of the contact person who will be the company's direct representative for the job at the library. The company contact needs to hear when things are going well, as well as when things are not meeting your expectations. It is advisable to request that the same person or crew be sent to the work site on a regular basis so they can become familiar with the building and what tasks are expected of them. This way you will have consistency in the cleaning of the facility by an outside crew. Emphasis on these areas by the facilities manager or the library director will ensure a good management-worker relationship.

1.6   How to Manage Maintenance Contract Work

When it seems desirable to use private vendors rather than having staff on the library's payroll, maintenance is an area that can be appropriately contracted out because it is not direct client service. We heartily disapprove of contracting out any library professional function that directly serves the public.

There are four types of contracts for maintenance work. These are: labor; material; labor and material; and labor, material, and overhead.

In a labor-only service contract, there usually is an existing supervisor on the library's staff who will be the liaison with the service contractor. All that is then required of the contractor is to bring in the laborers who will do the work using the library's cleaning supplies and equipment under the library's supervision. In the agreement, there is usually specification of the tasks to be done; the expected compensation for laborers; rules, library policies, and safety codes laborers will be expected to follow. Also specified in the agreement are resources provided by management, such as supervision and support.

In a material-only contract, the library is supplied with a particular item and in a specified quantity. It is delivered at intervals and in quantities as needed, with an agreed price per unit. It is usual for the library to agree to buy a minimum amount from the supplier to receive a specific price or else pay an additional fee. This type of contract applies to consumables, such as fuel oil.

In a labor and material contract, the library might require supplemental work crews to work along with the in-house staff because there is a temporary need. In the case of a large capital project, this might be the type of contract that is used. An in-house supervisor may be adequate, but labor and material for this period may be assigned to a contractor.

In the fourth type of contract, where labor, material, and overhead are considered, your library may not have any staff who are assigned to do the custodial work. It is then totally assigned to a vendor through a contract. In this situation it is imperative that the library director set out clear levels of expectation during the contract negotiations, so that it is understood from the outset what is expected for the dollars expended. The written agreement should stipulate the number of workers who will be sent to the job site; if a supervisor will come from the company; whether work will be done when the library is closed; what liability insurance covers workers; how often service is to be rendered, and so on.

This agreement should spell out the scope of services required and the performance measurement that will be used. Do not wait until the end of the contract period to find out about major deficiencies in the work schedule. The director should meet with the company on a regular basis to evaluate work performed and to keep the custodial program on target. This will make the situation a win-win one for the library and the contractor, and of course, for the public.

1.7   Guidelines for Training Maintenance Personnel

Training, in one form or another, begins the day an employee is hired and continues throughout his career with the library. The first training experience should be the general new employee orientation to the workplace. The new employee brings to the organization certain experience, skills, and knowledge that he already possesses, but no familiarity with the new surroundings or the work rules, policies, and practices. Orientation should cover subjects in the policy and procedures manual, all work rules, and a clear job description. The organizational chart of the library should be made available so that employees know to whom they report. A floor plan of the facility should also be provided whether one person in the library is charged with personnel matters or a central personnel office is part of your system. The orientation should also include presentations from the staff explaining the benefits offered, union contracts, safety rules, off-limits behavior (such as smoking), and other information. Zero tolerance for discourtesy to other staff or clients and sexual harassment of any type should be covered.

If the library is going to have maintenance employees on staff, every effort should be made to have appropriate training opportunities. These may not necessarily be offered by the library. There may be other workers, perhaps in the municipal system or within a business in the city, who also need this training. Sharing the training is a cost-effective way of making these opportunities available. Some of the likely topics include: back safety, blood-borne pathogens, drug and alcohol abuse, fall protection, fire safety, heat stress, motor vehicle awareness, workplace violence protection, sexual harassment policy, and Equal Employment Opportunities (EEO) policies.

1.8   Housekeeping Standards

There are three basic standards that apply to housekeeping operations: the frequency with which the tasks need to be done; the amount of time that is necessary to accomplish the tasks; and the quality of the completed work. These three standards need to be matched to each particular operation, taking into consideration the age and the overall condition of the facility, the particular functions that are to be performed, and the level of staffing that is required to accomplish these standards.

Task-frequency standards are specific target periods for completion of particular housekeeping activities. For example, it may be that the carpet in a particular office needs to be vacuumed only once a week, while the carpet in the main entry level needs to be vacuumed daily. A conference room may need to be cleaned after each use, especially if there are multiple users daily. By setting specific frequency standards for completing tasks, unnecessary ambiguity can be avoided. The end results are spaces that are neat, clean, attractive, and inviting.

The following is a suggested list of items that need cleaning in a library and the frequency with which they should be cleaned.

Figure 1–5
Housekeeping Standards Checklist

The facilities manager should develop a quality control program that will assign the task frequency, the time that each task is intended to take, and any other element that is specific to the particular facility.

In the following pages, we have included a general outline of the types of tasks that can be incorporated into the housekeeping standards of a library building for specific areas.

Mechanical Rooms

Floor surfaces should either be swept or cleaned with a wet or dry vacuum cleaner. Do a damp mopping at least once a month. Whenever outside contractors perform work, especially in an area such as this, they should be made aware of what cleanup is expected of them.

Rest Rooms

These areas should be cleaned on a daily basis. Toilets, urinals, basins, changing tables, and countertops should be cleaned with a disinfectant solution. Dispensers should be restocked daily. Mirrors, tiles or wall surfaces, and partitions should be cleaned at least weekly and more often if there is evidence of soiling.

Floors

Carpeted floors throughout the building need to be vacuumed daily. In addition to removing dirt, this extends the life of the carpeting. Hard or tile floors should be swept or dry mopped daily. The frequency of wet mopping, scrubbing, and buffing of these surfaces will depend on the amount of traffic they endure.

General Building

By setting specific frequency standards for completing various tasks, ambiguity can be avoided. These frequencies, of course, will vary according to the type and use of the particular areas.

All recycling bins and wastebaskets need to be emptied on a daily basis. Dusting of book shelves, bookcases, cabinets, and furniture needs to be done at least weekly.

Window sills, radiators, moldings, and so forth also need to be dusted weekly. Depending upon the ventilation system, blinds, ceilings, and other areas may need to be done weekly or monthly. Drinking fountains should be cleaned daily. Front door glass and lobby partitions and glass also need to be cleaned on a regular basis. Elevators floors also have to be mopped or vacuumed. Various surfaces need to be dusted and polished. Regular inspection and preventive maintenance must also be done to major equipment.

1.9 Housekeeping Space

There should be at least one dedicated, fully equipped space on each floor of the library for storing equipment and supplies for the maintenance program. A minimum of 60 square feet is recommended. It should have adequate lighting, independent ventilation, electrical outlets, hot and cold water, a utility sink, and storage shelves. This room should be secured so that only authorized personnel have access to it. There should be a garage or shed area to store large equipment, such as a lawn mower, snowblower, rakes, and so on, as well.

1.10 Assessing Your Maintenance Program: Evaluating Staff and Costs

Maintenance activity is dynamic, not static. Conditions change, equipment changes, people change, and needs change. Day-to-day problems arise and have to be solved quickly. Oral feedback from all staff concerning conditions, changes, and problem areas is a good source for suggested action. A written report system is another way that documents the need for corrective action. However, unless the person who is responsible for the program initiates the appropriate changes, there will be a problem in meeting maintenance objectives.

Certain factors should be considered in evaluating maintenance systems. The first of these is work performance. If the contractor or staff know what the expectations are, and they have been sufficiently trained in using good methods, their skill and effort will be evident. The second factor is adequate coverage for the work that is to be done. If preplanning of work has been properly done, coverage should not be a problem. If it is, check to see if staffing has been done effectively. If your maintenance program is experiencing delays, has equipment breakdowns, or is short on supplies, it may be that effective scheduling has not been done.

And, finally, you should be able to determine the cost per hour, which is the average labor cost to produce one planned hour of work, and see how that fits into the overall amount of money you have budgeted for labor costs. A control system of this type results in fewer emergencies, which will also lowers costs as well as eliminates headaches.

A written report that documents these areas will allow the manager to determine trends, spot weak areas that might need improvements, and analyze the situation before any further actions are taken.

The written report should include the following information.

- Actual labor hours
  —hours spent on planned work
  —hours spent on unplanned work

—any delays that prohibited work from being done (example—a power outage)
- Materials used
  —supply use for inventory purposes
  —equipment used
- Backlog
  —work that needs to be done but is not complete
- Cost analysis
  —amount of actual labor time versus what was planned
  —use of materials against standard
  —any cost variance between what work was expected to cost and what it actually cost

Evaluating the performance of staff in the facilities management area usually includes comparing the time that workers actually took to complete a task against actual industry standards, as well as the quality of the work performed. These can be found in a volume such as *Maintenance Manager's Standard Manual* by Thomas Westerkamp. (See Useful Reference Materials in Chapter 9.) Lower performance will occur when workers have little skill or do not put enough effort into the tasks at hand, or if there is poor planning or scheduling of work. If workers have the benefit of good planning and efficient scheduling, as well as effective training and adequate supervision, performance should be good. In order to keep the library's facilities management program as cost effective as possible, the manager has the responsibility of looking at productivity. Evaluation must consider the performance of workers in terms of both skill and length of time worked. Only then, will the manager be able to have a clear picture of how well the program is working at the library.

Figure 1–6
Sample Cleaning Services Contract

Agreement for Cleaning Services for the Anytown Public Library

This Agreement, made on the _____ day of_____, 20__, by and between the City of Anytown, hereafter called the "City," and Cleaning Experts, P.O. Box 554, Anytown, USA, hereafter called the "Contractor."

Whereas the City is desirous of engaging a contractor for cleaning services at the Library;

Whereas the Contractor is in the business of providing such services;

Now, therefore, the parties mutually agree to the following:

1. **Agreement of the Parties**: The City hereby contracts for, and the Contractor hereby agrees to provide, cleaning services under the supervision of the library director of the Anytown Public Library or a designated representative.

2. **Scope of Services:** The Contractor shall perform all of the duties and responsibilities in accordance with the general cleaning requirements.

3. In the event of any dispute concerning these services, the City's judgement shall be final.

4. This Agreement shall begin on _____ and end on_____ unless extended or terminated.

5. The City shall pay the Contractor:

   a. Payment of $_____ shall be made in a lump sum per week.

   b. Payments to the Contractor shall be for actual service provided and invoices shall be submitted before the tenth of each month, when payment is due.

6. It is understood that under the Agreement, the services of the Contractor shall be as an Independent Contractor and not as an employee of the City, and that the persons employed by said Contractor are employees of the Contractor and not of the City.

7. The Contractor shall assume full responsibility for conforming to all requirements for proper cleaning services and the City will be held harmless from any and all claims that could arise in the provision of such services.

8. The Contractor assumes full responsibility for all cleaning personnel. The Contractor hereby agrees to immediately discipline or discontinue the use of cleaning personnel in the performance of this Agreement when the director of the Anytown Public Library notifies the Contractor that a cleaning person's performance is unsatisfactory.

Figure 1–6
(Continued)

---

9. **Insurance:** The Contractor shall provide and maintain a Certificate of Insurance for the duration of the Agreement.

10. **Termination:**

    a. The City or the Contractor might without cause terminate the Agreement within 30 days following written notification to the other party.

    b. Should the Contractor be unwilling or unable to provide the service, and is unwilling or unable to resume the service within 36 hours, the City may seek another vendor.

Contractor:_____   Date:_____

City:_____   Date:_____

Witness:_____

2 Supplying Utilities and Energy Management

Note:

Three main areas of consideration for utilities in a facilities management program are telecommunications, electrical power, and water and sewer service. While the current environment has made us acutely aware of the need to upgrade telecommunication systems, unless one is considering an expansion to the facility or a new building program, it is easy to take running water and electricity for granted in this country. However, a good facilities manager needs to be aware of what roles these utilities play in the day-to-day operation of the library and what disasters might happen if there is interruption of any one of these.

2.1   Electrical Service

Prior to discussing electrical service, it is extremely important to understand that electricity is a dangerous element because of the possibility of shock or electrocution. Some facilities and even licensing and accrediting organizations require electrical problems be taken care of by an electrical professional. The authors believe the same. The following information should be helpful to avoid a problem or to understand why something has occurred.

If you are in a library that has been in existence for some time, it is important that you contact your local electricity provider and ask it to work with you to do an audit of your building and its needs. However, not all electric companies will do energy audits because of liability or a lack of staff. Sometimes it is necessary to retain an energy consultant for this process. With the amount of computing and networking we are adding to our services, it is critical to know if your building has been wired appropriately to handle this electrical load. The company will make recommendations that will protect you from overloading circuits and preventing damage to both equipment and the facility.

Be sure your consultant tells you the type of service you have, including the amps, volts, and phase. The facilities manager, the director, and other supervisory personnel must know the location of the electrical panels. This is extremely important because the panel box is the first place to check to see if a fuse has been blown or a breaker tripped.

Newer libraries will most likely have breakers; older buildings tend to have fuses. Whatever the case, these "go off" when the number of amps passing through a circuit exceeds the maximum allowed. This stops the flow of electricity to that circuit. When this happens, it is important that you follow these steps. First, you must find out what caused the problem (were there too many plugs in an outlet, was a wire frayed, did water drip on an appliance?) and correct it. Once you have determined the problem and corrected it, you can then reset the breaker by simply flicking the breaker switch from off to on.

If you have fuses, replace the blown one. This should be done with the exact same type and amperage fuse. Fuses usually come in 15, 20, 25, 30, or 40 amps. They may be made of glass, porcelain, or plastic. Some are inserted by pushing, while others are threaded or screwed in. The size of the thread and the length also vary. Again, replace fuses with like fuses.

A library may have more than one panel box and all panel boxes might not be in the same area. Find out the location of all of them. It is also important that each fuse or breaker within a box be labeled as to what circuit, outlet, appliance, or fixture it protects. This labeling is necessary for a number of reasons. If you have a problem, the labeling will help identify the circuit in question. Also, if you need to do some work on a particular circuit, you can close only that area without disturbing another area or circuit. It is a good idea to lock the panel box if it is visible to the public. This will prevent anyone from harming himself or doing damage to your equipment or system. Fire codes restrict storing anything within three feet of the panel box.

Energy conservation is another factor that concerns electric distribution companies. They may recommend upgrades of systems that are more flexible and therefore more efficient to operate. These include heating and air cooling systems as well as lighting systems. Insulation, too, can be a great way to produce energy savings. Energy providers are encouraged and sometimes required to help users with energy-saving suggestions. Deregulation of the electrical utility companies has helped to stimulate this assistance.

The utility company or a certified lighting contractor will conduct an energy audit and energy assessment of your current lighting system with your approval. It will review your electric bills and inspect all fixtures, switches, and outlets. The company will look at your schedule and peak hours of operation as well as do a walk-through of your library. After it has compiled this and other information, it will suggest a plan or program to help you. These suggestions should do the following for your library:

1. reduce your energy costs
2. reduce maintenance costs
3. maintain an optimum light level
4. improve the quality of library lighting
5. help increase employee productivity
6. contribute to a cleaner and safer environment

After reviewing the energy audit plan, these are some of the questions you may want to ask of contractors.

1. During the upgrading process, will your library have any disruption of services?
2. Is up-front capital required for this upgrade?
3. Is there a grant program available from the utility company?
4. Do the lights that are being suggested cause interference with computer screens?

5. Does the program suggest use of room sensors for smaller, less frequently-used areas?
6. Does your library own all equipment for the upgrade or will you lease it?
7. How long will it take to complete the retrofit?
8. Are any permits required? Who will apply for them?
9. Is the lighting company responsible for the removal of old ballasts and bulbs?
10. Does the company have insurance to cover not only its own workers but the librarians and the library patrons and the building as well during the upgrading?
11. Can rebates be claimed for retrofitting existing fixtures or using energy-efficient fixtures in new buildings or in renovation projects?

The preventive maintenance program comes into play with the electrical system because clean filters, appropriately adjusted belts on equipment, as well as simple things like the cleaning of boilers and chimneys will also make a difference in energy use.

Outdoor signs, monuments, walkways, and parking lots are very often illuminated by lights that are turned on by a photocell. When it gets dark in the evening, the cell senses the lack of light and turns on the illuminating source, whether it be a floodlight or a street light. This requires periodic changing of the photocell. If all outside lighting is wired from the same panel, a single timer can work all of the lights. Present-day technology allows different lights to come on at different times and provides the capability to program them to change automatically when the seasons change.

The library director must be able to communicate the electrical needs of the facility to an approved electrical contractor so that the installation and the continued operation of power and lighting functions is adequate to meet the library's needs.

If the library experiences power irregularities, there are several things that can be checked to correct the problem. The facilities manager will want to consider the type of electrical load that is being placed on the system, the times of day when the electrical needs are the greatest, and if there are differentials during different seasons of the year.

In preparing budget numbers for utilities, be aware of the demand for electricity that your building has. The demand is the maximum rate of power that is used by nonresidential electric utility customers for a specified interval in a billing period. Peak energy usage is usually measured during the regular weekday (from 8 a.m. until 5 p.m.). Kilowatt hours (1,000 watts per hour) is the standard that is used to measure the amount of electrical power that is consumed.

Figure 2–1
Sample Energy Audit

April 1, 2000

Village Library
100 Farm Road
Anywhere, USA 00000

RE: ABC Utility Company Energy-Efficient Lighting Improvements at:

100 Farms Road
Anywhere, USA

200 Meadow Road
Anywhere, USA

Solutions LLC is pleased to present Village Library with a comprehensive energy-saving lighting improvement proposal for two (2) Village Library locations in Anywhere, USA.

Solutions, working as a preferred energy services provider for ABC Utility Company, has prepared a comprehensive lighting system improvement proposal utilizing an approved, small business, energy-efficiency program that includes the following features and benefits:

1. two-year zero-percent financing for the total capital improvement cost from ABC Utility Company. The Village Library does not pay any costs up-front for any improvements

2. all financing charges conveniently included as part of your monthly electric bill, resulting in easy-to-track positive cash flows for Village Library

3. significant reductions in ongoing energy and maintenance costs, resulting from the upgrading of lighting systems throughout the facility

The Solutions proposal includes the following easy steps for implantation.

1. ABC Utility Company has reviewed and audited all of Solutions' proposed lighting systems upgrades to ensure that each lighting measure qualifies for energy saving and meets ABC Utility Company lighting system criteria.

2. ABC Utility Company has approved Solutions' proposal and qualifies the project to participate in its zero-percent financing program. This program allows the Village Library to finance the lighting system improvements for up to 24–months with zero-percent financing and utilize the energy savings to finance the capital improvement costs.

Figure 2–1
(Continued)

3. Solutions performs turnkey installation, project management, and commissioning of all lighting system improvements covered under the proposal.

4. ABC Utility Company will perform final inspection and sign-off on the commissioning of all qualified capital improvements.

Solutions is pleased to have the opportunity to develop and implement the proposed lighting system upgrade proposals for both locations in Anywhere, USA. The attached proposal provides the opportunity to significantly reduce long-term energy and maintenance costs. If you have any questions regarding the attached proposal, please call me. I look forward to hearing from you.

Sincerely,

William Anyone,
Solutions

I. *SUMMARY OF UPGRADES AND ASSOCIATED SAVINGS*

Lighting System Upgrade Summary

Solutions performed a detailed audit, walk-through, and energy assessment of the current lighting systems located throughout 100 Farm Road and 200 Meadow Road. A summary of the various locations reviewed and covered under the proposal is as follows.

The detailed audit included a review of all lighting applications located throughout the facilities. Areas of opportunity included but were not limited to:

Lobby Areas	Stairwells	Utility Rooms
Hallways	Bathrooms	Storage and Locker Rooms
Enclosed Offices	Conference Rooms	Stack Areas
Open Office Areas	Staff Room	

A sample of existing lighting systems and proposed upgrades is summarized below.

Figure 2–1
(Continued)

Existing Lighting Systems	Proposed Lighting System Upgrade	Average Reduction In Energy Use
4 Lamp, 40–Watt T12 Straight Tube Fluorescent Lamp Ceiling System and Magnetic Ballast	2 lamp, 32–Watt T8 Retrofit with Electronic Ballast and State-of-the-Art Reflector System	68%
75–Watt Incandescent Lamp	18–Watt Compact Fluorescent Lamp	76%
Exit Sign: 2 15–Watt Incandescent Lamps	New Exit Sign w/2 0.9–Watt LED Lamps	94%
400–Watt High Bay Metal Halide Fixture	New 220–Watt Fluorescent Biax Fixture	53%

II. *PRICING AND PAYBACK ANALYSIS*

Below is a summary of improvement costs, available utility incentives, and associated payback analysis.

	100 Farm Road	200 Meadow Road	Total
Total Installed Cost of Measures Including: Labor, Material, Disposal Costs (*), and Sales Tax	$49,794	$5,151	$54,945
Less Utility Incentives	($21,715)	($1,962)	($23,677)
Net Project Costs	$28,079	$3,189	$31,268
Annual Energy Savings	$14,219	$2,261	$16,480
Annual Maintenance Savings			$ 2,018
Total Annual Savings			$18,498
Simple Payback			1.7 Years
Return on Investment			59%

(*) Includes proper disposal and manifestation of PCB ballasts, lamps, etc.

Figure 2–1
(Continued)

III. *ANALYSIS OF CASH FLOW*

Below is a ten-year (10) cash flow analysis that illustrates the benefit of ABC Utility Company's zero-percent financing program and the impacts of future energy savings.

Year	Net Cash Flows	Net Present Value
1	$2,066 (*)	
2	$3,661 (*)	
3	$16,480 (**)	
4	$16,480 (**)	
5	$16,480 (**)	
6	$16,480 (**)	
7	$16,480 (**)	
8	$16,480 (**)	
9	$16,480 (**)	
10	$16,480 (**)	
TOTAL		$77,565 (***)

CONCLUSION: Implementing the proposed lighting improvements will yield a present value improvement in cash flows of $77,500 over a ten–year period.

(*) Represents net cash flows from energy savings, financing costs, and maintenance savings

(**) Represents energy savings with no associated financing costs

(***) Discount rate of 10%

Energy and Maintenance Savings Analysis

Annual Energy Savings:

Source: Utility Company Analysis Program
Documents (See Appendix A)   **SAVINGS**

Project No.	Annual Kwh	KW Demand	Annual $ Savings
100 Farm Road	115,242	32.80	$14,219
200 Meadow Road	17,245	6.19	$2,261
	132,487	38.99	$16,480

Figure 2–1
(Continued)

Annual Maintenance Savings:

Fixture Type	Fluorescent Fixtures	Incandescent Lamps	High-Bay Fixtures	Exit Signs	Total
No. of Fixtures	403	21	24	47	
Annual Turnover	25%	200%	50%	100%	
No. of Changes/Yr.	100	42	12	47	
Hardware Cost per Replacement Labor Hours per Unit Labor Cost per Hour (1)	.25 $15	.25 $15	.50 $15	.25 $15	
Annual Hardware Svgs (2) Annual Labor Svgs	$600 $375	$84 $158	$300 $90	$235 $176	
Total Annual Svgs	$975	$242	$390	$411	$2,018
Total Annual Maintenance Svgs					**$2,018**

(1) Average labor rate per hour

(2) Hardware cost for lamp replacement

Analysis of Monthly Cash Flows

Below is a graphical display of the monthly cash flows of implementing Solutions' proposed lighting improvement proposal.

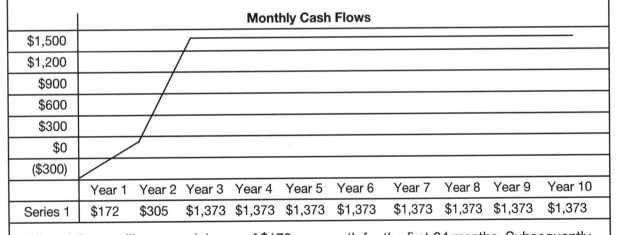

Monthly Cash Flows

	Year 1	Year 2	Year 3	Year 4	Year 5	Year 6	Year 7	Year 8	Year 9	Year 10
Series 1	$172	$305	$1,373	$1,373	$1,373	$1,373	$1,373	$1,373	$1,373	$1,373

Village Library will save a minimum of $172 per month for the first 24 months. Subsequently, Village Library will save $1,373 per month from reduced energy use and costs.

2.2 Uninterrupted Power Source

It is a good idea to have controls installed on equipment that could be damaged by power surges. These controls are universally known as uninterrupted power sources (UPS). They are especially important to have to protect computers, telephone service lines, and other electrical equipment.

These suppressors and UPSs come in many sizes and capabilities. They may be as small as and look similar to an extension cord. Some are larger and can resemble your computer server (tower-type model). Whatever the look, make sure you get those that are able to provide you with the protection you need.

You can protect a single computer, a modem or line, or a network of computers. When deciding what to purchase, know what you want to protect. Power protectors will indicate the amount of joules and watts and the number of outlets supplied; a UPS will list the run time.

Look for the following features and ask these questions when purchasing UPS equipment:

1. Does the UPS provide zero transfer time?
2. Does the UPS have automatic voltage regulation that corrects under- or over-voltage?
3. Are modem amd fax also protected?
4. Is there software available that shuts down your computers during prolonged blackouts?
5. Does the UPS provide computer-grade 120v AC power?
6. Will the UPS save open files?
7. Is there insurance available from the manufacturer if the surge protector or the UPS malfunctions?
8. Is the UPS data line enhanced for protection while connected to the Internet?
9. Is the protector equipped to stop RFI/EMI noise from harming connected equipment?
10. Does the protector have an indicator light to show protection status?

2.3 National Electric Code

The National Electrical Code (NEC) is a detailed document, revised regularly so it is in line with current trends, discoveries, and developments. Provisions in the code provide for a fail-safe system for wiring. The engineers and corporations represented by the code formulators devise wiring schemes to make things work in a manner they hope will never go wrong. However, the code also makes provisions for safe dissipation of potentially lethal amounts of electrical power. This is a document intended by insurance companies to reduce the number of fires and accidental deaths that could occur from faulty wiring. The local power company and fire department are good sources of safety information in the electrical area. In our libraries, especially with the added demand for power because of the use of computer technology, it is critical that we get expert advice.

2.4   Smart Energy Savers—Lighting

It is important to consider the right source and the proper amount of lighting for the particular activity that is being performed. Key factors in determining interior lighting needs are the average age of the people who will be working in the area, the contrast with the background (painted surfaces, for example), the type of work that will be performed in the area, and the need for accuracy. Lights can then be selected by their wattage, efficiency, color output, mounted height, location, and spacing. Exterior lighting is usually "fixed," that is, it is set in a light distribution pattern that cannot be adjusted. Lights are usually mounted on walls or on poles and aimed downward onto surfaces. The choice depends upon the amount of illumination that is needed.

Three maintenance activities that reduce light loss and thus save energy are repainting on schedule so that the reflected light is at its maximum, scheduling of lamp and fixture cleaning, and scheduling lamp replacement.

2.5   Air Conditioning and Ventilation

One of the major systems that keeps buildings habitable as well as comfortable is the heating, air, and ventilation system. In most libraries, specialized equipment is used for these functions, is often referred to as the HVAC system. The system includes chilled and hot water, cooling towers, steam absorption units, and mechanical refrigeration systems and boilers. In some smaller libraries, room air conditioners, identical to the units that are used in homes, may be used.

Many of the headaches associated with air conditioners come from too many people adjusting the thermostat too often. The facilities manager and her designee should be the only people who adjust the controls so that problems are avoided. It will be impossible to please everyone with the air temperature, and different buildings have their own quirks about heating and cooling. However, an expert can help the library design a plan that will keep the facility reasonably comfortable.

The authors offer the following suggestions:

1. Lock the thermostat to prevent anyone other than the facilities manager from setting the controls.
2. Clean all filters periodically.
3. Set thermostats seasonally and automatically.

4. Set evening temperatures (nonworking hours) lower than during working hours if this is efficient for the HVAC system and results in a savings.

5. If someone complains that his office is too hot or too cold, check the balancing of your system. Check the flow of heat or air through ducts and the amount that is allowed to flow to a single room.

6. Check the air returns on a periodic basis.

7. If your library is closed from Friday afternoon until Monday morning, consider an alarm for both high and low temperatures. This will tell you if your system is malfunctioning while you are away from the building. This can usually be connected to and monitored by the fire alarm company.

8. If your units are operated by gas, a gas detection alarm is also highly recommended.

The facilities manager should have on hand the operations manual provided by the manufacturer of the chiller (air conditioning unit). The manual will explain in detail all the operating steps. It also has recommendations about start-up and shutdown procedures, tests (such as for oil levels) and the frequency they should be done, filter replacement schedules, and the like. Because of the complexity of the equipment, it is recommended that the ongoing operation and maintenance of these systems be handled by certified professionals.

2.6   Water Supply

In some buildings, old water service lines might still be causing problems. For many years pipes and solder had a heavy lead content. It is important that you check the pipes at the library so you know whether they contain lead and should be replaced. When it became known that lead is a poisonous substance if ingested, the U.S. Environmental Protection Agency (EPA) set a standard for safe drinking. This is 50 parts per billion, but the EPA has proposed reducing the level even further to 10 parts per billion. The Safe Drinking Water Act of 1974 (amended in 1976) is federal protection for safe public drinking water. It also bans solder in waterline connections. Water supplies that are more acidic will dissolve lead faster than those that are alkaline. Hot water will dissolve more lead than cold water. Recommendations for the improvement of drinking water systems include the replacement of plumbing repairs with nonlead solder. It is also a good idea to test water levels for lead, and if readings are between 5 and 10 parts per billion, to replace them.

Water from well sources may also bring other problems. It is critical that care is taken so the source of the well water is not in danger of being polluted from any toxic source.

Filters should be changed regularly, according to the manufacturer's recommendations, to ensure that the drinking water is safe. If you have taken all of these steps to ensure that drinking water available is at safe levels, and you have not overseen the access point, there may still be problems. In public buildings, it is important that water fountains are sanitized on a daily basis. You should also make sure that their refrigerant operation is kept in good working order and that water is not allowed to collect in the basin and become stagnant. This is another example of preventive maintenance that could avoid health problems.

2.7   Plumbing

The plumbing system in the building, including all of the piping, valves, and fixtures, is another area of concern. In addition, the plumbing system may be integrated with the heating and air system, depending upon the type of heat that is used. This plumbing system helps regulate the flow of water, oil or natural gas, air, or a combination of these substances into the equipment so that it can run properly and do the job for which it was intended. As is true with many of the other areas discussed, the best way to handle plumbing maintenance is to avoid problems.

Preventive maintenance of pipes and drains is not difficult. However, they do require consistent monitoring. We would not recommend the use of chemical treatment to keep drains open. Rather, boiling water poured down them every few months will serve to clear them just as well. Leaky faucets almost always stem from the fact that water can force its way past the washer even when the appliance is fully turned off. A worn-out washer can cause an excessive loss of water and be disturbing at the same time. Simple replacement of washers will help save water and stop annoying leaks.

Figure 2–2
Checklist for Plumbing Operations and Repairs

1. The water supply brings water from the reservoir or well into the library. Once at the facility, the water enters the building through the main supply line from the meter. The meter is usually located at the road or where the supply enters the building. Check this meter at regular intervals to be sure it is operating and not leaking.

2. Familiarize yourself with the location of the water main. This is important because the main is where you shut off the flow of water to your building in an emergency. Practice how to close and open the shutoff. Also, find out if there are any additional shutoffs for both hot and cold water. If a sink doesn't have its own hot and cold water shutoffs, install them.

3. Label all shutoffs. Describe what they turn off and to what fixture they are connected. Sometimes, the basement, mechanical room, and boiler room have a number of shutoff valves that turn off water, gas, steam, and so on. Pipes that carry those elements should also be labeled. The American National Standards Institute recommends proper pipe identification and has set up color-coding guidelines. These are: red for fire protection materials; yellow for hazard to life and property; green for low-hazard liquids; blue for low-hazard gases. In addition to labeling all shutoffs, document their location and keep this information in a place accessible to all supervisors.

4. The drain-waste system carries waste products or used water from the library to the city's sewer system or the library's septic system. Most often the system is gravity-designed. A waste system has a normal pitch if for every horizontal foot of pipe there is between 1/4 and 1/2 inch pitch. On occasion, pumps must be used to allow the waste to flow. If you are using pumps, know what they are pumping. We also suggest that you have a spare pump in case the original pump fails. If a pump fails, it might not be discovered until there is a backup of waste material. Because of this potential hazard, we recommend the pump be alarmed in case of failure. This will warn you before any nasty mess occurs.

5. A venting system is one of the most important parts of any plumbing system. This system stops any gases that could be harmful from entering the library. It carries away sewer gases and maintains proper pressure within those pipes. Without proper venting, the rest of the plumbing would not work because the flow of water and waste would be inhibited. Vents are often located on the roof of the facility.

6. If you see water leaking from hot and cold water turn-on or from any valve, you might have to repack that part. When fixing a leaky faucet, first shut off the water supply to the fixture. If the water is leaking hot, you may only have to change the washer on the hot water turn-on. Some sinks have a single-handle faucet and this requires a special ball-type washer fixture. Most regular water faucets are called compression faucets. It is recommended that you tape chrome or plated fixtures before using a wrench to repair them. Remove the small screw to the handle. Pull the handle off. Remove the packing nut from the stem. The small rubber O-ring should be changed. Take off the old washer by turning the brass screw counterclockwise. Replace the old washer and secure by turning the brass screw clockwise.

2.8   Boiler Maintenance

Proper boiler maintenance is essential to ensure reliable operation of the boiler and its auxiliary equipment. This will also ensure maximum possible equipment life, as well as maximum operating efficiency and safety. Failure to maintain boiler equipment might lead to safety hazards and accidents. Failure to have feed water treated can cause corrosion. Equipment can also overheat or corrode.

Good boiler maintenance is ongoing maintenance. Some equipment performs a number of tasks. There are gas units that provide not only heating but also air-conditioning. Some units not only heat rooms in the winter, but the same boilers provide hot water throughout the year. Still other units have separate burners for heat and hot water. It is important to acquaint yourself with the equipment and how it functions, so you can identify problems and have them repaired rather than be left with no heat.

A good maintenance routine would include these points.

1. Check to see if your burner company has a maintenance program.
2. Clean the boiler or furnace yearly, including all burners, hot water tanks, and exhausts.
3. Where filters are used, change them seasonally.
4. Change nozzles yearly.
5. Inspect transformers periodically.
6. If the burner is oil-fired, don't let the tank go below 1/4 full to prevent sediment from clogging the flow of oil.
7. If the system is a hot-water system without an automatic feed, add water to the system as needed.
8. Check all circulators annually.
9. Calibrate all thermostats prior to the spring air-conditioning season and the fall heating season.
10. If the building has radiators that need to be bled, do so annually at the start of the heating season.

The questions below can help diagnose potential problems.

1. Do you smell burning oil? This might mean that too much fuel is igniting—a rich mix of fuel and air.
2. Do you smell gas? A possible gas leak or a pilot might be out. Call the gas company immediately.
3. Do you hear noises? This could be a worn part or a bad motor or circulator.
4. Do you hit a reset button and the burner motor goes on but the fuel does not ignite? This could mean you are out of oil or are not getting a flow

of fuel to the burner. It might be a clogged fuel line or nozzle. A transformer might be defective.

5. Do you see soot? You might have a dirty chimney or clogged exhaust pipes. Too much fuel burning at one time is another reason this might happen.

6. Do you see smoke? This is a concern. Unless you can determine the source quickly, call the fire department immediately, as smoke can indicate a fire and is life threatening. The problem might not always be a serious equipment failure, but the smoke can cause serious injury or death. Smoke can be caused by many possible things: a belt might be stuck; a nonlubricated part is overheating; the fuel mix is burning dirty; or the exhaust is backing up.

Figure 2–3
Heating System Troubleshooting Guide

Gas Furnace

Be sure the filters stay clean. At the first sign of cycling, squeaking, abnormal noise, or reduction of air volume, a service technician should be called. These are early warning signs of future problems.

Oil Furnace

This is the same as for gas, but additionally, if your unit runs out of oil, in most cases the filter and the nozzle should be replaced. If your equipment shows any signs of unusual cycling or sooting, this may be a sign that you have a bad heat exchanger. Call a technician before major sooting occurs.

Fan Coils (Air Handlers)

Check the filters to see if they are clean. You should recognize any odd noises and realize that these are usually signs of pending component failure. Early reporting can save your system. If the fan coil has air conditioning, the cooling coil and the condensate lines should be cleaned annually.

Hot Water Boiler—Gas or Oil

Make sure at the time of start-up that all air is vented from the system. Check the boiler gauge frequently to insure temperature is being maintained. Boiler temperature may vary based on outdoor temperature. Lubricate related circulators and check controls to be sure they are working properly.

Steam Boilers—Gas or Oil

Steam pressure must be maintained during all conditions. Check water-level indicator to be sure the boiler maintains proper water level. Clean and test the water feed as required. Blow down the boiler periodically to rid it of excess sediment. Check steam taps to ensure they are opening and closing as designed. If all the above is done annually, you will increase efficiency, save energy, and minimize system failure.

Condensing Units—Outdoors

Look for dirt buildup on coils. If unit cycles in short intervals, this may indicate a low level of gas. Report any strange noises as soon as possible to service company. This may save on extensive repairs.

The above troubleshooting guide should be used by the facilities manager in coordination with the annual preventive maintenance plan. It is recommended that there is a maintenance plan on the equipment and for service. This will minimize major breakdowns and help you predict and, to some extent, control annual operating costs.

2.9   Underground Oil Tanks

Underground oil tanks are another area of potential concern with heating systems. These tanks have a life span of 20 to 30 years. Some communities and some states require by law the replacement of underground oil tanks within a specific time frame (usually every 25 years). Check your local and state ordinances to see if your community requires replacement of underground oil tanks within a specified period of time.

Old metal tanks should be replaced by double-wall fiberglass tanks for maximum protection and safety. Because of the potential of environmental damage due to leakage, all tanks should be tested annually. Audible alarm systems can be installed with the units that will indicate if any leakage has occurred. Because of the potentially hazardous conditions that can result from the leakage of oil, it is recommended that expert advice be obtained. Replacement of the tanks should be done in cooperation with the city's engineering or public works department, taking special care that water supplies are not endangered. Carrying insurance on the tank to protect you from financial risks associated with a leaking tank is highly recommended.

Figure 2–4
Checklist for Fuel Storage Tanks

1. Is fuel consumption, compared to the same period in the previous year, extremely high?

2. Do you smell an odor of fuel outdoors?

3. Is the area by the tank unusually soggy?

4. Is the earthen material near the tank settling?

5. If you answer "Yes" to any of the above, call a professional and have the tank checked.

Figure 2–5
Costs Associated with Replacement of Underground Tanks

1. complete removal of the old tanks not only from the ground, but from the premises

2. removal of any contaminated soils

3. dumping fees associated with the removal of the above

4. new tank to meet the size requirements

5. new soil, including all support materials, backfill, and any covering soil

6. plumbing to drain tank

7. plumbing and installation

8. paving, if appropriate

9. soil testing

10. engineering fees, including the design

11. permit fees

2.10   Smart Energy Savers—Heating and Cooling

It is a good idea to have an energy audit or assessment of the facility performed so that you will be able to determine if there are any problems that can be solved to reduce energy consumption. This can even be tied into the lighting audit that was mentioned earlier, especially if an outside energy consultant is used. This is a sensible first step in understanding and determining if there is indeed any waste of energy at your facility. What will result is a report that offers suggestions to eliminate energy waste.

Some of the suggestions may include regular service to equipment, as well as preventive filter changes and chemical treatments. These are proven methods of reducing energy charges. To be most effective, however, the audit should include alternative suggestions for actions that can be taken, along with their costs, so that the library has a choice on the way to proceed.

Humidity levels may also affect energy costs, and clearly humidity is an issue with the materials that we have in our collections. Mold and mildew will grow on books and other surfaces if humidity levels are too high. In addition, the air quality will not be comfortable for staff or patrons. Some systems require that heat run simultaneously with the cooling system in order to control humidity levels. This would result in higher fuel costs. Other systems may not require this method, but need additional dehumidifiers placed throughout the building. These run on electrical current, and unless they are attached to a drainage system, will require manual emptying by the maintenance staff. This has an impact on the cost of operation, but the dollars are well-spent in terms of preserving the collection.

There are three factors that have the greatest effect on the amount of energy that is used within buildings. First is **temperature,** specifically the difference between the outdoor and the indoor temperatures. Hot air rises. If it rises to the ceiling and there is no insulation, the heat will escape. Heat can move in any direction and it will always move to an area of lower temperature. The greater the difference in temperature and the less resistance a material offers to the flow of heat, the faster that the heat will be able to circulate.

R-value is the term that is used to express a material's ability to retard the flow of heat. Window glass has a low R-value; walls usually have a higher value, which is dependent upon the amount of insulation. Doubling the R-value by adding insulation is one of the efficient ways that can slow the flow of heat. Building and fire codes may address the recommended value.

Temperature is measured in degree-days. This is a term that combines both temperature and time and serves as an index of the amount of energy that it takes to heat or cool a building. Degree-days are calculated by taking the high and low temperatures for the day, adding them, and then dividing the sum by two. That number is then subtracted from 65. Sixty-five is the usual starting point, because research has shown that a building needs neither heating nor cooling to maintain this comfortable level.

The second consideration determining energy use is the **condition of the building.** If the building is what construction workers term as "loose," there are cracks around doors or window frames or around the foundation. The windows or the doors may also be loose or warped. All of these contribute to air-leakage losses.

The third area to consider is the **actual condition of the heating and cooling systems.** The inside of the furnace may be covered with soot, which will then reduce the amount of heat that is delivered. If oil-burner nozzles or gas orifices are clogged, if air inlets are not properly adjusted, or if the chimney is obstructed, there may also be heating or cooling problems. The controls may need adjustment so that the furnace will fire when it should and shut off when it should. Filters on the air conditioner or furnace may need cleaning or changing. All of these problems mean that you will be getting less for your heating or cooling dollar than you are paying for.

Saving energy means getting the maximum amount of energy out of the fuels you buy. First, your furnace should be set up and maintained to deliver as much heat as possible for the fuel it burns. Second, saving heat means keeping heat within the building in the winter, or out in the summer, for the longest possible time so that less energy will be required to keep the building at a desired temperature. Use window coverings for this purpose. Third, saving energy means tailoring the equipment to the task. You should choose all equipment sensibly so you will get the required results without unnecessary expenditures of cash. Checking the temperatures of the water heater and other appliances is crucial for conserving energy.

There is no single set of conservation measures that will work in every building, nor a single step that will always result in a significant savings. You will want to pay special attention to those measures that will yield the greatest savings per dollar of cost.

2.11 Telecommunications

Various types of equipment can be vitally important in the delivery of library service, for communication with coworkers, patrons, suppliers, and other colleagues. Patrons especially expect you to use the latest equipment and to make reaching you easier for them, and rightly so. Communications tools have vastly improved in the last few years and they are much more flexible than ever before. They also have many more features so, as library directors, we have many more choices to make regarding telecommunications products.

Telephones systems can either be leased or purchased. In Chapter 4 there is a detailed example of a Request for Proposal for a telephone system. This will more fully indicate some of the options available. Depending upon the size of your library, we recommend that you talk with several vendors. For very large systems, it would be appropriate to employ the services of a telecommunications consultant to assist you.

Some of the features available today include: mutimedia messaging (integrated voice, fax, and p.c. connections), automatic attendants, voice mail, programmable phones, indicator lights, hold keys, redial, display windows (caller i.d.), speakerphones, hands-free operation, and multiple-line options.

The selection of a long-distance carrier is another choice that the library will have to make, especially if there are significant amounts of calls of this nature. A toll-free line might also come into the mix.

Cell phones, while initially expensive, are becoming more and more affordable. They offer great flexibility and are of great use with outreach services, especially bookmobiles, homebound service, and satellite operations. It is important that you shop around and check rates. The library may be eligible for special contracts because of its status as a nonprofit or a municipality. Again, we would recommend checking several selections.

Pagers are another communications tool that are helpful for the facilities manager and outreach workers, and for security guards. They are available with an audible sound or a vibrating message. They are a way of keeping in touch with individuals who are away from the primary site. Contracts similar to those of cell phone service are available. The authors recommend that you consider the use of cell phones instead of pagers for a variety of reasons: Cell phones are now nearly as inexpensive as pagers; some phones act as both pager and walkie-talkie, in addition to the phoning capabilities; if security guards are paged, you are at the mercy of a paging company to relay your message—the loss of time might be critical in an emergency situation; a phone allows the individual to call or talk, not just listen.

Depending upon the size of the library, the phone system can have many variables. The following are some suggestions to consider when deciding on new phones. It should also be noted that in some types of structures, cell phones do not operate well. Walkie-talkie units or a combination of cell phone and walkie-talkie are other options.

Figure 2–6
Phone Control Options to Consider

- Allow all phones to dial out to local emergency numbers.

- Allow all phones to call internally to each other.

- Not all phones need to call long distance. Restrict those that you feel shouldn't.

- Roll over as many lines as possible to prevent the public from getting a busy signal too often. Do take into consideration that librarians need to make calls out, so have a sufficient number of outside lines, too.

- Not all phones need to be multiline phones. Single-line phones are fine for some staff and are less expensive. Consider the responsibilities of the person when you make decisions to put single-line or multiline phones in different areas.

- Purchase phones that have transfer and hold capabilities.

- Large phone companies have many customers all calling for service at the same time that you need service. Some problems can be corrected from a central location, while others will require a service call from a technician. Options available to you include priority service guaranteed by a service contract or the use of a local independent contractor. Often these contractors are retired from phone companies and are willing to make their services available less expensively and on a more timely basis. This option does not compromise skill or technical knowledge.

2.12   Internal Intercom Systems

Internal intercom systems are useful to make public announcements, especially in emergency situations. There are relatively inexpensive units from about $200 to very sophisticated systems that run into thousands of dollars. Consult with an audiovisual specialist, who will be able to help you select a system based on your needs, taking into consideration the size of your facility and the anticipated use of the unit.

2.13   Internet Service Providers (ISPs)

Internet Service Providers (ISPs) typically lease carrying capacity from telecommunications providers, who own the wires, fiber optics, and switching equipment that carry Internet traffic. ISPs then resell the service to customers, using a combination of their own local equipment and others' to provide connectivity.

At the local level, large ISPs build networks consisting of hundreds of points-of-presence (POPs) connected by high-speed, dedicated, leased lines. POPs consist of routers, which direct traffic; call aggregators; servers; and frame relay or ATM switches. Smaller ISPs may lease connectivity and even POPs from larger ISPs rather than build their own network.

There are other ways to access the Internet than just the wireline telephone system. Cable companies and satellite services offer Internet access in some areas. Wireless services are another option. Fiber-optic lines offer much faster access than traditional dial-up modems. All of these start out on a different type of network, but are linked to the Internet at some point. Telephone companies also offer broadband Internet access over upgraded telephone lines called DSL (see 2.14).

If your library is part of a municipal, county, or state system, it is our recommendation that you contact them to explore the possibility of working together before selecting an Internet provider. The options and "frills" that ISP offer are often much enhanced in proportion to the number of users, for example, free e-mail, business cards with the e-mail address, the ISP's icon on the desktop, rebate deals, and so on.

You will want to evaluate the speed of the service, its reliability, and its ability to handle periodic traffic surges. In addition, many services provide you with assistance in creating Web pages. Many ISPs also offer Web-hosting services.

2.14   Digital Subscriber Line (DSL)

DSL stands for Digital Subscriber Line. This allows for the transmission of voice, video, and data over copper telephone lines at incredible speeds. DSL provides bandwidth that can be up to four times faster than a T1 connection. There are various forms of DSL. ADSL (Asymmetric Digital Subscriber Line) is the most popular form. This supports up to 8 Mbps bandwidth for downloading and up to 1 Mbps for uploading. The asymmetrical nature of ADSL technology makes it ideal for the Internet, video–on-demand, and remote local area network (LAN) access. The installation usually requires the use of a voice/data splitter, so that voice and data transmissions are separated. DSL connections utilize a bandwidth of up to 1.2 MHz and enable data speed from 128 Kbps up to 6.144 Mbps. Libraries considering installation of wiring should discuss which type of lines would be most efficient for their purpose with a consultant from their local provider, if the city does not have an expert on staff.

SDSL (Symmetrical Digital Subscriber Line) delivers high-speed data networking over a single pair of copper phone lines. This is done at the same speed in both directions and it is important if the library will be engaged in a large amount of video conferencing.

HDSL (High bit-rate Digital Subscriber Line) delivers high-speed data networking of 1.544 Mbps over two copper pairs and up to 2.048 Mbps over three copper wire pairs. VDSL (Very high bit-rate Digital Subscriber Line) is the fastest of the DSL technologies. Downloads can be delivered from 13 to 52 Mbps and uploads at 1.5 to 2.3 Mbps over a single pair of copper wires. However, this is limited to a range of 1,000 to 4,500 feet.

3 Providing the Right Environment

3.1   The Inside Environment

The environment of a facility should be designed to be attractive, appealing, and approachable for those who use it, and it should be conducive to the productivity of the employees. The environment or atmosphere says a great deal about the library and often is what creates that lasting impression for the first-time visitor.

3.2   Lighting

Internal lighting is an important feature of the atmosphere created within a building. It is an essential element of good working conditions for both staff and users alike. Our lighting needs have changed over the years with the introduction of new equipment, especially microfilm readers and computers. Well-designed lighting makes the workplace brighter and more attractive. A feeling of safety and well-being also comes with bright surroundings and this contributes to better employee-customer relations, a greater interest in work, and fewer mistakes. Good lighting helps people who have sight problems. It reduces eye-straining, which can cause stress and fatigue.

The amount of light necessary for comfortable visualizing is dependent upon four conditions:

- size and location of the objects to be seen
- contrast with a background
- amount of time there is to focus on an object
- brightness

Taking these things into consideration, the needs for the strength and the type of lighting will differ in different locations of the library, and with time of day. For example, you will want bright, but diffused light to prevent glare in study carrels, fluorescent bright lights in book stack areas, and bright, direct lighting in parking areas. Your goal is to provide proper illumination, while at the same time preventing glare that makes reading or working at computers difficult. If your library is considering a major change in lighting patterns, we strongly recommend working with a knowledgeable consultant and/or electrician who can advise you about some of the modern options that are available. There are six general categories of fixtures that should be considered for indoor use: indirect, semi-direct, direct, general diffusing, semi-indirect, and direct-indirect. When your building was designed, the architect probably considered the amount of both direct glare and reflected glare that these types of light would produce within your structure and made the selections based on the type of work that was planned for particular areas. If usage for these areas has changed, the facilities manager has the responsibility of recommending other fixtures or replacement lamps that can have the best effect for the intended use. In any event, relamping is considered to be an ongoing maintenance issue. This should be done at regular intervals, with gradual replacement, so that the lighting level of the overall building has not had a chance to be reduced. This process will help to control the safety and health issues that may result from improper levels of lighting.

One of the best sources for information on lighting needs in libraries is the volume *Libraries Designed for Users: A Planning Handbook*, by Nolan

Lushington and Willis N. Mills Jr. In it, the authors state the function of lighting is not only to help people find materials to borrow, but also to provide adequate lighting that will limit eye fatigue in areas of the building that are intended for long-term use. They also recommend the use of task lighting. With task lighting, the light fixtures are directly related to the type of work that will be performed in a particular area of the building. Ideal library lighting includes a variety of appropriate lighting levels with minimum glare and minimum brightness of the light fixtures.

There are three basic types of fixtures that are available for lighting libraries.

> *Incandescent*: The bulb life of this type of lighting is often less than 1,000 hours. It is expensive compared with the other types of lighting. However, incandescent lighting presents good color and is comfortable for long periods of time.

> *Fluorescent:* With fluorescent lighting there is a high lumen output per watt of electricity. It is not unusual to have bulbs last over 20,000 hours. Warm, white fluorescent bulbs or balanced white (sunlight) provide relatively good color rendition that will be comfortable for reading for long periods of time. The least expensive type is strip fluorescent lighting with quiet ballasts.

> *High Intensity Discharge (HID):* These are usually mercury vapor or metal halide light bulbs. The advantage of these lights is they will burn twice as long as fluorescent bulbs and provide high lighting levels per dollars of electricity consumed. Color rendition is not as good as incandescent or fluorescent bulbs, and the ballasts tend to be quite noisy.

It is important to remember that with high lighting levels glare is often produced. Glare reduces the ability of the eye to contract, and therefore the ability to see clearly is reduced. In order to cut glare, light must strike objects from many directions, a process that is technically known as inter-reflection. Diffusion lenses are the solution to cutting the glare that is caused by direct artificial light. The relative location of fixtures and reading surfaces can also reduce reflected glare.

In any event, light levels of 30 to 60 foot-candles are needed in reading areas.

Figure 3–1
Lighting Checklist

- Avoid sunlight in long-term use areas. Sunlight is unpredictable and difficult to control and may cause long-term damage on printed materials.

- Select lenses carefully to diffuse light and prevent glare. Acrylic opalescent lenses of molded plastic work well.

- Place fixtures to minimize the brightness of the ceiling and reflectance caused by light striking

- Limit light intensity variation in small rooms.

- Use low-intensity light in nonreading areas.

- Install fixtures that burn cool. Plan scheduled group relamping to economize.

- Avoid glare and reflection by careful selection of light locations and fixtures.

- Remember that white ceilings and walls increase light.

3.3 Air Quality

Air quality is another area of concern for the indoor environment. Studies conducted by the National Institute of Occupational Safety and Health indicate that over half of the indoor air quality problems are due to inadequate ventilation. Other major causes are contaminants such as dust, vapor, exhaust, pollen, smoke, and even building furnishings and fabrics. Better ventilation can reduce these. Other maintenance issues that should be checked so ventilation remains good are: filters, storage areas, fans, insulation, chillers, humidifiers, pipes and leakage, nonoperative air louvers, and air ducts. Serious liability due to illness and safety hazards can result if these are left unattended.

In some older structures radon can become a problem. Radon is a radioactive gas that occurs naturally from the breakdown of uranium. You cannot see it, smell it, or taste it. Radon accumulates in an enclosed space. Levels depend upon the building's construction and the concentration of radon in the underlying soil. Since radon is a gas, it moves easily through small spaces in the soil and rock upon which foundations are built. Radon can seep into a building through small cracks in concrete floors or walls, floor drains, sumps, joints, and tiny cracks or pores on the hollow-brick walls. The amount of radon in the air is measured in picocuries of radon per liter of air or pCi/L. The Environmental Protection Agency recommends that a long-term test (over 90 days) should be done. The levels should be 4 pCi/L or lower. A qualified contractor should be called in to perform the appropriate tests and to make recommendations that will lower the radon rate in the structure.

3.4 Water Quality

Water quality, especially for drinking, is of concern if the library has old water service lines. Until 1930 or so, these lines were made with a high-lead content, or soldered with such. If this is the case, they should be replaced. Until then, bottled drinking water should be provided instead.

3.5 Humidity Issues

Humidity control is another issue that is crucial to the operation of a library where so many materials must be stored. Library materials, especially those made from paper, are especially susceptible to damage from high humidity. If heating and cooling systems are not controlling the humidity of the building to an appropriate level, you will begin to see mold and mildew growing on your collection. On the other hand, if conditions get so dry with the heating system you have, you might find that book bindings dry out and paper becomes brittle. The facilities manager will want to check the balance on the system to see if that is the problem. A relative humidity between 30 and 40 percent year-round is the accepted standard. There are various options available to add moisture to buildings. One of the simplest ways is to use a melted drum type of humidifier. This does do the job, but it is important to make sure that it is maintained monthly. Another method is to use some form of steam injected into the air supply system. This must be done with careful control so that too much moisture is not added.

Dehumidification is required when there are prolonged hot and humid spells. With temperatures over 80°F with high humidity or periods of heavy rains or floods the growth of mold spores may result. There are four accepted methods of prevention. The most commonly used is a condensation prevention or ventilation system. This means the use of a cooling system that is in operation whenever outside humidity is too high. In some systems, it may be necessary to run the heating system simultaneously in order to reheat air enough for comfort. Secondly, chemical moisture barriers may be of use in a limited area. With these, air is pushed over moisture-absorbing chemicals and is dried with heated air. Portable dehumidifiers can be utilized to take out moisture. These units usually need to be emptied by hand, but may sometimes have a hose that can go directly into a drain. They can be used in confined areas for short intervals; however, they cannot be expected to carry out the job for the entire building. Fans are the fourth main method of controlling humidity. They can be put on exhaust when the outside air is cooler than the inside air, but not too humid. They are also used to replace the hot "day" air with the cooler "night" air. In addition, in some situations, double-pane glass, sometimes referred to as thermophane, is helpful in preventing condensation. Insulation of walls and a vapor barrier are other methods often employed to control moisture. Thermostats might be the cause of an area that just "doesn't feel right." These can be calibrated so that they are more efficient.

If these simple solutions prove not to work, then it may be necessary to have additional work done to the system or to add additional dehumidifiers, placed in strategic areas, to control the problem. The goal of the program is to maintain the temperature and the humidity of the building at a fairly constant set point during the entire year. Trouble happens when there is ongoing fluctuation of temperature and humidity.

3.6   Outside the Library—The Grounds

The old adage reminds us that first impressions are important and lasting. By the time patrons enter your library, they have already formed an impression both of the facility itself, and of the people who run it, from the appearance of the grounds. That first impression or perception, whether it is correct or not, is the one that frequently stays with the patron, and it may color his visit and use of the library, as well as his interaction with the staff. The impact that the first impression makes underscores the reason it is so important to have a comprehensive grounds maintenance program in place. Well-kept grounds project an image of a well-run facility. A well-maintained exterior is another element in providing a healthy and pleasant working environment for the staff and visitors alike. Poorly maintained driveways, parking areas, and sidewalks, as well as overgrown bushes and low-hanging tree limbs are threats to the health and safety of people.

Good maintenance practice promotes the health of the various trees and shrubs, decreasing the need to replace them, and preventive measures can extend the life of paved or masonry surfaces, thus reducing the frequency of replacing them.

To be effective, the grounds maintenance program must be tailored to meet the requirements of your facility. As with anything else we do in managing our libraries, we must consider the level effort and the funds that are available in setting up the program.

3.7   Establishing Grounds Standards

In order to achieve and maintain the desired level of quality in the appearance of the grounds, standards must be developed. This will be the basis for determining what activities are to be performed and how frequently. Without established standards, what might be considered to be a requirement by one person might be seen as unessential or extravagant by another. Establishing a grounds inspection program is the place to start. With it you will determine the baseline of how your grounds currently appear and you will be able to establish standards. Future inspections will determine how well the standards are working.

Periodic inspections are useful to identify problems so they can be corrected before they become serious. Check whether plant maintenance and surface maintenance are being done according to the established standards. Time is another factor that should be considered in establishing standards. You need to estimate the average time that is required to perform a given task under normal operating conditions. There should also be a schedule of frequency of performing tasks depending on the time required to accomplish them.

Keeping the grounds maintained means that all of the parking areas, trees, lawns, flower beds, hedges, and shrubs need to be cared for. Lawn care includes mowing the lawns during the growing season and removal of leaves in the fall. Litter control and disposal is performed daily all year long. In addition to trimming, trees and shrubs also need to be watered on a regular basis, as well as sprayed and fertilized.

In addition, snow removal from the sidewalks and parking lots is considered under this plan. A priority list of areas to be cleared should be developed. Sidewalks, and entrances to the building, as well as all parking areas must be included. Special attention should be given to all areas where there are stairs, as inadequate removal of snow may result in icing. Salting and sanding must be done on an "as needed" basis.

3.8 Duties of the Groundskeeper

There is no one answer on how the outdoor upkeep of a facility is to be done. Some libraries have an individual on staff who has that responsibility; other libraries contract it out to a private company; still others have dedicated volunteers who do the work. Much of the work is heavy physical labor, and those responsible must have knowledge of weather, as well as trees, shrubs, flowers, and grasses that are on the property. They also must know the types of chemicals that should be used for plant care as well as insect and rodent control. A person assigned this task must also have the know-how to keep the equipment that is used to maintain the grounds in good repair, or to know who is available to do so.

The primary duties for groundskeeping are planting and maintaining lawns, shrubs, flowers, and trees. Repetitive work that is required during the growing season is cutting, pruning, trimming, watering, fertilizing, and controlling weeds. Duties outside the growing season include pruning shrubs and limbs from trees, raking leaves, and preparing and protecting plants for cold weather. These duties do require the use of a wide variety of tools and equipment, including common small power tools, mowers, clippers, sprayers, spreaders, rototillers, salt spreaders, pruning saws, chainsaws, and chippers.

Preparing a groundskeeping organizational plan is time consuming, but worth it. This plan outlines the work that would be done over a year-long period and the staffing, product, and equipment needs that are necessary to fulfill it. This gives the director an overview of what needs to be done and is helpful in scheduling. It is also quite useful in the preparation of the budget.

Outside work is sometimes interrupted by bad weather. With forethought, staff can be shifted to other appropriate responsibilities so that personnel time is still wisely spent. Alternate plans for bad weather days are a must! These might include sign making, indoor plant care, or repair of furniture. Other types of repairs can also be done: tool sharpening and lubrication or replacement of broken parts on a lawn mower. More work will get done in peak outdoor weather if tools are kept in good condition.

3.9 Planning for Unexpected Weather

There should be an emergency plan for unexpected severe weather. Snow, wind, and heavy rainstorms make extra work. Planning can be assisted by information from local weather services, but you should have equipment and supplies on hand well before there is a need to use them. You should think about what materials, tools, and equipment should be ready and who will be on hand to do the work. What outside contract services are available—for snow removal, de-icing, brush or tree removal? What should be done for personnel safety if confronted with broken windows, downed power lines, or stalled vehicles? The various types of emergencies should be listed in a document and discussed with personnel before an emergency hits. Call lists with names and phone numbers should also be included as part of the plan. The library will benefit from having everyone in the organization working from the same plan, avoiding the considerable confusion that these types of situations might generate.

This type of planning for weather situations that we cannot control will help you manage the crisis quickly and safely.

3.10 Lawn Care

Dealing with common lawn problems at the outset will improve the lawn's appearance, help minimize the need for specialized care, and prevent reoccurrence. Healthy lawns are more than just pleasing to the eye. They also help maintain a healthy and safe environment by cooling the area, replenishing our oxygen supply, filtering air, and reducing noise pollution.

Important basics for maintaining a good lawn include having a regular schedule to keep grass mowed at the desired height (you should never remove more than one-third of the grass blade); mowing grass when it is dry for a cleaner cut; keeping mower blades sharp; and alternating mowing patterns to avoid uneven wear on the lawn. Mulching is another important step that improves the fertility of the soil.

> *Bare Spots:* Winter damage may cause bare spots that are noticeable in the spring. Small spots will usually fill themselves in as the lawn begins to grow. Raking and aerating the lawn will let more oxygen into the roots and promote growth. Fertilizer will also help. Larger spots should be filled in by seeding with a good grade of grass seed, which should be covered with a mulch until it begins to grow.

> *Lawn Moss:* In areas that are very wet or poorly drained and where there is a lot of shade, lawn moss will thrive. Improving the drainage and thinning trees to admit more sun are permanent solutions to the problem. Chemical products can also be applied, but these are temporary solutions.

> *Fungus:* If your lawn exhibits discoloration or general thinning, a fungus should be suspected. A combination of a fungus control chemical and a fertilizer alleviate this problem.

Insects: There are many types of pests that can damage a lawn. A broad-spectrum insect control product should be applied with the fertilizer application. This will even control such common pests as fleas and ants.

Lawn Weeds: There are many products on the market to assist the gardener with this problem. It is best to use a weed-control product mixed with an application of fertilizer so that the bare spots left by the weeds will fill in with grass.

An established lawn can survive a long time in most climates However, proper watering schedules will keep it green and healthy.

Mowing in the spring and fall can be done when the grass is $1\frac{1}{2}$ to 2 inches high. In hot periods of summer, our recommendation is that grass should be 2 to $2\frac{1}{2}$ inches high. By cutting often, you will be able to leave the clippings on the ground and return the nutrients to the soil without forming thatch. A mulching mower is an excellent way to recycle grass clippings, leaves, and other yard waste, and return it to the soil, while still keeping the lawn looking groomed.

3.11 Shrubs and Border Plants

Once planted, shrubs are very hardy, and with a minimum of care, will last for many years. Planting conditions for these are best in the late spring or early fall.

Textures and plant sizes vary. You should select those that will fit into the look you want to achieve for the grounds. Arrange plants that require similar soil conditions and care together, while mixing types for the sake of appearance.

When making decisions about what to plant, it is important to visualize the mature size of the plant and plan for proper spacing. The look of the building will change with the addition of these greens, and you want to be sure that you have made selections that will work with the design, not against it.

Shrubs require a lot of water and soil that has been loosened to allow the roots to settle in. New shrubs or transplants need daily soakings for a few weeks so they can get established. Regularly loosen the soil around them during the growing season so the soil is aerated and weeds cannot get established. Trimming shrubs should be done to prune away unhealthy or broken branches and to promote the growth of healthy ones.

3.12 Tree Care

Trees not only enhance the aesthetics of your facility, they can also provide energy savings. This is especially true when their location provides for shade outside areas with windows. Planting smaller trees may be done by someone on staff, as long as careful thought has been given to the location of underground cabling and piping. Larger trees should be installed by a professional through a nursery service.

Many of the same techniques that are used to maintain healthy shrubs also apply to trees.

However, their root systems are far more extensive, and aeration and watering need to extend out for quite a distance so that the supply of air and water is plentiful.

In addition to watering, trees need occasional pruning to prevent disease and damage and to promote healthy growth. All broken branches or damaged bark should be removed and covered with tar to seal it from invasion by water or insects.

Weak, broken, or diseased tree and shrub limbs should be removed in the fall when the branches are bare and damage is more easily seen. Dead trees should also be removed. If left unattended, they can fall unexpectedly when wind, ice, and snow further weaken them, creating a serious hazard. Conditions to look for are cracks in branches or trunk bark, especially in the "y" between two heavy branches, and large bare patches where bark has fallen away or has been rubbed off by two branches rubbing together. Evergreens, such as spruce and pine, should not be pruned in late fall, nor should spring flowering plants. Pruning stimulates growth, and new shoots might be too soft to survive the winter. It is better to prune in the spring, after blooms are gone.

3.13   Other Outdoor Concerns

There are other areas of concern for the area surrounding the library that have to do with both the aesthetic appearance of the facility and the safety of individuals who will be using the library.

Lighting is the first of these concerns. It usually falls upon the facilities management staff to make sure that all the lighting is working properly, especially at entrances and exits; that bulbs and ballasts are replaced as needed; that a timer or photocell is installed to ensure that lights come on as soon as darkness falls; and that signs and parking areas are well illuminated. While we will not go into all of the types of lighting that are available, since this is more appropriate for a volume on architecture or construction, the facilities manager should make sure that the library's lighting is adequate as well as energy efficient. Consideration in the construction phases should be given to the number of hours that the bulbs and fixtures are expected to last as this will have an impact on the replacement schedule that the maintenance staff will oversee, as well as on the operating budget. If upgrades to the lighting patterns are being considered, we would recommend that the facilities manager check with the local electrical utility provider. There are often rebate and incentive programs designed to maximize energy efficiency that can help underwrite this type of upgrade.

In areas where public transportation is not frequent, and when a library is located in an area that is best reached by automobile, parking is always an issue. It is important to know local zoning regulations and the number of parking spaces city officials deem necessary for a facility of your size. Accessible parking for handicapped individuals is also a must. The maintenance crew will need to keep the parking area clear of debris, trash, glass, leaves, and snow or ice. The pavement will need to be checked for cracks and faults, and repaving recommended when necessary. The lines indicating parking spaces may also need frequent repainting, perhaps on an annual basis. These are items that will need to be added to the general facility management plan.

Snow and ice removal is crucial for the safety of all individuals, both employees and patrons, who will be using the building. Entryways, stairs, walkways, paths, ramps, and drives as well as all parking areas will need to be treated. You may want to check with local officials about the compound they recommend to reduce sliding. It may be sand only, salt only, a combination of both, or some other mixture for your particular area of the country.

The roof is the area of a building that is more exposed to the greatest environmental extremes than any other building component. In addition, for every dollar of damage that is done to a roof, there will also be an additional amount of dollar damage done to the building contents. Therefore, it is important that the roof is well designed, that it is properly installed, and that frequent inspections and routine maintenance are done so that it will provide the maximum performance.

Depending upon the architecture of the building, the library may have gutters installed. Gutters serve an important purpose because they prevent water from running across windows and doors and down the sides of a building. They also channel water away from the foundation and prevent erosion of soil. Gutters are made of aluminum, steel, or vinyl, which gives them a long life. However, they are not maintenance free.

If water backs up severely enough to run over the backs of the gutters, there is a great possibility of damage to the roof sheathing, eaves, and fascia boards. Periodic cleaning is an economical and relatively painless way to prevent water damage from inoperative gutters.

3.14 Pest Control

Both the inside of the library and its grounds may need to have pesticides applied to control insects, rodents, and plant growth. It is important that the chemicals used are carefully selected and applied by an individual who is knowledgeable about the substances, as well as aware of any applicable laws.

The Environmental Protection Agency (EPA) has the responsibility of overseeing individuals who are certified to apply pesticides. At libraries, there is a need for pest control for ornamental planting and turf. Inside the library, it is important to make sure that preventive measures are taken to control pests that might invade structure and books. Roaches and mice are naturally attracted to glue and this makes books vulnerable. At our library, we learned that roaches seek out warm places when a circulation staff member opened some returned videos and the creatures paraded across the desk! Kitchen areas and staff lounges also attract insects, including ants, to unwashed soft drink containers that are waiting to be recycled.

Standards and qualifications may vary slightly by state, but in general, all states require following the guidelines for pest control that have been established by the EPA. Persons who apply pesticides must demonstrate a knowledge of chemical labeling; follow approved safety procedures; be aware of the environment and take precautions to protect it; know how to identify various types of pests and be able to make the proper selection of the pesticide that is most suited to extinguish each of them; and be skilled in the use of the necessary application equipment and techniques. In addition, if it is at all possible, application of chemicals should be done when there are no staff around, or as few as possible, and the building well ventilated before reoccupation. Warning signs of the pesticide's application should also be posted. Because of the serious nature of pesticides, it is important that a person who is certified to provide the application is hired. In most cases, this means that a qualified, outside contractor, not a library employee, be assigned the task.

Pest control issues do extend to a broader area than the insects that may be attacking plants and shrubs. Rodents (mice, rats, and even squirrels and raccoons) may be a dangerous problem. These animals can become rabid and cause injury to people. They also have the tendency to nest and make their way into openings in walls, garages, basements, and so on. Bats also like to squeeze their way into roof flashing, overhangs, and garages. Keeping the facility in good repair will eliminate an invasion of any of these pests.

Close and careful attention should be given to eliminating conditions that are conducive to pest infestation. All pests need food, moisture, and harborage. By eliminating one or more of these, we make it more difficult for pests to survive. Reproductive rates are also slower when conditions are not conducive for survival. Food, paper goods, and other supplies should be visually inspected upon arrival for cockroach infestation. Corrugated boxes should be unpacked and items stored properly. Shipping cartons should be disposed of as soon as possible. Sanitation and elimination of moisture sources are also important preventive steps.

Ants and many other pests can be excluded by caulking and patching cracks in walls, floors, and sidewalks. Branches of trees and shrubs should be trimmed away from the building to eliminate pest access. Organic mater, wood debris, and other trash should be raked away from the foundation whenever possible.

The pest control technician will identify and make recommendations about

Figure 3–2
General Pest Management Plan

Library Name _____

Address _____

Phone Number _____

Pests to Be Controlled

Pest control services include treatment for cockroaches, ants, winged termites, incidental invaders including bees and wasps, flies, and other arthropod pests. Populations of these pests that are located immediately outside a specified building pose a possible infestation problem to that building and must be treated.

The "Main Street Library" will be inspected by the XYZ Pest Control Company for the purpose of identifying potential problem areas that may be contributing to pest infestation within the facility. XYZ will make recommendations for corrective measures that must be implemented and will develop a comprehensive, integrated pest management control plan. This plan will include the visual inspection of potential problem areas. All methods of pest control, including sanitation, monitoring for pest populations, mechanical and biological control, and the judicious use of pesticides will be employed as necessary. The selection of pesticides used will be based on a predetermined hierarchy, which will utilize the least toxic products as the first choice.

XYZ will submit recommendations for corrective measures in writing to the library director or facilities manager prior to application of any pesticides. The company shall be responsible for scheduling this application on a mutually agreeable time frame with the library.

Records

The company agrees to make a written "Pest Control Service Record and Pest Inspection Report." These forms will be given to the library director and will be kept on file.

Pest sighting logs will be maintained by the library staff and turned over to the pest control technician at the beginning of the service call. This log will include the specific information as to the location and type of pest if known. This will serve as a tool to facilitate communication between the library and the pest control company.

Monitoring

Glueboards will be used to monitor pest populations and activity. Visual inspection of these will help the pest control technician to identify specific areas of infestation and to assess the need for further action or preventive steps.

Figure 3–2
(*Continued*)

Ants and many other pests can be excluded by caulking and patching cracks in walls, floors, and sidewalks. Branches of trees and shrubs should be trimmed away from the building to eliminate pest access. Organic matter, wood debris, and other trash should be raked away from the foundation whenever possible.

The pest control technician will identify and make recommendations about occasional invaders. These include drain flies, fungus gnats, earwings, spiders, centipedes, bees, and wasps. If they pose a health threat they will be treated accordingly.

Rodents

In addition to creating structural damage, mice and rats are known to spread organisms such as salmonella, tapeworm eggs, hantavirus, and leptospirosis. In an effort to prevent and eliminate rodent populations, it is important that conditions favorable to their survival be reduced as much as possible, or better yet, eliminated. The following are some appropriate suggestions:

- Action should be taken to mouseproof the facility by plugging holes in the foundation and walls. Steel wool can be used as a temporary patch while awaiting permanent repair. Special attention should be given to areas where sewers and drains enter a building.

- Water runoff should be directed away from the building. Drains should be screened with $\frac{1}{2}$-inch hardware cloth to prevent rodent access and kept free of debris to reduce the puddling of water.

- Weather stripping on doors should be repaired or replaced to reduce gaps to less than $\frac{1}{4}$-inch. Exterior doors should have automatic closing mechanisms installed and remain closed whenever not in use. Loading dock areas should be clean and free of debris, and doors should remain closed as much as possible.

- Trees, shrubs, vines, and brush should be trimmed away from the building at least 12 to 18 inches to allow access for pest control technicians to monitor and place bait or traps as necessary. Grass should be mowed and trimmed.

- Dumpsters should be in good condition with all doors closed and drain holes capped. They should be located away from the building on a paved surface. Trash should be contained.

- Storage areas should be managed using a first-in, first-out program. Inventory should be kept on elevated pallets or shelving that is 12 inches or more away from any wall.

Figure 3–2
(Continued)

Precautions should be taken with the type of pesticides and the methods that are used for rodents. Tracking powder is one element that would cause difficulty in a library setting. The pest control company will want to make sure that if used, this substance cannot be blown by drafts into the air circulation system and that it is kept away from all areas used by personnel and patrons.

All outside vendors should be prepared to provide documentation that their services fall within the accepted standards that are established by the state's environmental protection agency. If a license is required in your state, the contractor should provide you with a copy for your files. A certificate of insurance is another document that should be on file. It will outline the range of liability that the company has for its services and products. If the library is signing a contract for services, these materials must become a part of the legal file that is kept on the company.

occasional invaders. These include drain flies, fungus gnats, earwings, spiders, centipedes, bees, and wasps. If they pose a health threat they will be treated accordingly.

Other types of pests that are not insects but may be unwanted visitors in your library are bats, raccoons, and skunks. Bats have the ability to squeeze their body into small spaces near roof overhangs, garage doors, and chimneys. They seek shelter as the cold season arrives and hibernate over winter months. In some parts of the country raccoons and skunks are becoming overpopulated and are having difficulty finding food, so they often forage in trash. Proper receptacles are necessary to prevent an invasion of these animals. Again, precautions are necessary because many of these animals become rabid, and could, in fact, inflict serious wounds on people who startle them.

3.15 Occupational Safety and Health Guidelines

The Environmental Protection Agency (EPA) and the Occupational Safety and Health Administration (OSHA) are active throughout the country, warning of health and safety hazards, establishing safety and health guidelines, auditing for compliance, and bringing offenders back into compliance. They issue findings and orders that each facility must comply with, and they enforce their orders with legal actions. In extreme cases, penalties can include fines and shutdowns.

Under the Occupational Safety and Health Act of 1970, employees have the following rights, among others:

1. to review copies of appropriate standards, rules, regulations, and requirements that the employer should have available at the workplace
2. to request information from the employer on safety and heath hazards in the workplace and precautions that may be taken and procedures to be followed if an employee is involved in an accident or exposed to toxic substances
3. to request that OSHA conduct an inspection if the employee believes there are violations of standards within the workplace
4. to be notified by the employer if the employer applies for a variance from an OSHA standard
5. to be advised of OSHA actions regarding a complaint and request an informal review of any decision not to inspect or issue a citation

These apply most specifically to the library as a workplace. Further information can be obtained by reading the actual legislation.

Employees also have obligations in regard to OSHA. These include the following:

1. to read the OSHA poster at the job site
2. to comply with all applicable OSHA standards
3. to follow all employer safety and health rules and regulations and wear any prescribed protective equipment if necessary
4. to report any hazardous conditions to the supervisor
5. to report any job-related injury or illnesses to the employer, and seek treatment promptly
6. to cooperate with OSHA compliance officers who may be conducting an inspection if they inquire about the safety and health conditions of the workplace

The rights and responsibilities of employees must be posted by the employer in the library. If the library has more than ten employees, the administration is then required to keep records of all work-related injuries and illnesses. Employees have the right to review the records. Included in the reporting are work-related injuries that result in death, lost work days, work or movement restrictions, unconsciousness, or medical treatment other than first aid.

4 Budgeting and Controlling Costs

4.1   The Finances of Facility Management

There are two types of budgets used for facilities management. They are the operating budget and the project or capital budget. Both of these should be tied to the components of the strategic plan that cover the facility. The purpose of the operating budget is to itemize each type of operating expense that is anticipated for the management of the facility. This type of budget is used to control material and supply costs, including the labor costs involved in the upkeep of the facility. The physical size of the building and its design will have an effect on the budget, as will the hours of operation. The more a building is used, the more it will need to be heated, cooled, ventilated, and cleaned, and have preventive work done. Routine repair, preventive maintenance activities, minor modifications, and building and equipment repairs are all a part of the operating budget. Previous expenses can be used to help forecast and estimate what the recurring costs will be in an operations budget.

The project or capital budget is used for a special, usually large, project. It, too, is included in the strategic plan as the library's long-range needs. The life span of items under this type of budget should be ten years or more. Examples are major construction, building additions, and roof replacements. Usually, these funds are not available in the annual operating budget and most often need a special appropriation from a major funding source.

Generally, forecasting for major capital needs is done for a period of five years or more so that the appropriate funding can be added to the city's long-term capital improvement plan. In many situations, the library may be required to raise a portion of the money. Sometimes, a natural disaster or a totally unexpected calamity happens, and there is need to secure funding immediately.

Cities usually will earmark some monies for this in a "contingency fund." However, in our experience, receiving the funds to cope with the pending challenge still requires background work and preparation before approval is given. You should familiarize yourself with your city's program and know what local, state, and federal funds might be at your disposal for the library facility. With state and federal funds especially, there may be different opportunities if funds become available for different projects. Examples of this are historic building renovation and bringing buildings into compliance for building, fire, or accessibility codes.

Two effective methods used to prepare budgets are the historical method and the zero-based method. Most budgets are based on the historical perspective. The library director or other individual who prepares the budget relies on the experiences from the previous year to estimate costs for the upcoming year. An inflation rate is added to the numbers, and the new budget request is ready. This method is relatively quick and there is a controlled amount of paperwork. It is a rational approach. However, if careful evaluation procedures are not in place, a past error may be perpetuated.

Zero-based budgeting follows the principle of developing the entire budget from the ground up with no reference to historical performance. Each budget item must be justified based on current needs and priority versus the funds available. Expenditures that are required by law, those that are not legally required, and new items are all considered with this prioritization approach. The major disadvantage of the zero-based budget method is that it is a much more time-consuming process, requiring more detail and documentation than a typical historical budget. This needs to be weighed with its major advantage, which is the better use of available funds and a clearer understanding of the objectives and goals of the organization on all levels.

4.2   Organizing for Budget Preparation

Before you can prepare a budget, it is important that you clearly relate the function of the maintenance plan to the mission of the library. You will need to continually focus on these objectives during the budget process so that it will remain consistent with the functions of the library. The following steps are useful in helping with the preparation of the budget.

The first step is the gathering of trend information for the past two to three years. You should ask yourself these following questions: How do this year's labor, material, and overhead costs compare with the last two years? What are the differences; are there increases or decreases and why? The next step is to compare this information with another department in your city, or perhaps with another library. Are there ways of improving costs by having some work done together? Are there other products or services that can help contain costs? Is it most cost effective to have maintenance staff on board, or would contracting the work out save significant money?

The next area that you will want to consider in the budget process is future plans. Are there anticipated changes in services or in the building? How will these increase the demand on maintenance services? An example might be the addition of Sunday service. At the very least, you will want to make sure the rest rooms are cleaned and supplies are refreshed, trash is emptied, and vacuuming done. All of these will cost more money, as will having heat or air conditioning on.

Computerized systems that track expenses and chart them against the approved budget enable you to look at variances on a regular basis. Variances can happen if budget projections were based on estimates or anticipated expenses. There are also unforeseen circumstances that could result in budget variances. This type of tracking system is good on a day-to-day basis, is useful in preparing future budgets, and saves time and administrative costs.

4.3 Purchasing Power

Another area of concern for the library director is the purchasing of supplies and equipment for the management of the facility. The director may have a great deal of experience and opportunity to talk with vendors for library and information resources, but it is not too often that she has experience in analyzing the costs for building supplies, equipment, and construction activities. We recognize that the library wants to get the most value for the dollar. To get the best services from vendors and contractors it is essential that the director develop the skills of purchasing management or delegate the responsibility to someone in the organization who has the ability to do so.

Specialized knowledge in purchasing will help your library avoid mistakes or oversights that will end up costing money. It will also reduce the time that is spent by less knowledgeable individuals in getting price quotes and other critical buying information, following up on orders that have been placed, and trying to expedite purchasing procedures. Purchasing information is also needed for the budget process, and the responsible person should be trained to keep records that will be useful documentation.

The director may find it is necessary to assign the purchasing of supplies and equipment to another individual in the library. It may not be the person who is in charge of overseeing the management of the facility. It may be someone whose functions are more clerical. It is critical that this person interact with whoever is actually maintaining the facility so that there are no misunderstandings.

Work cannot be done without equipment and supplies, and this process should be managed in the simplest and most efficient way. Communication about the types and quantity of products is important; the person who is doing the ordering must be sure that the items purchased will suit the needs of the person who is doing the work.

The person ordering must also give consideration to the amount of storage space available at the library. Sometimes purchasing in quantity will result in a better price, but if there is not a place to store the materials, it might not be a good idea to buy more. If materials are not stored properly, damage may occur, and there is a greater possibility that the items may be "taken" as well.

4.4 Areas of Concern for Purchasing

- cost/value analysis (when to repair, when to replace)
- preventing duplicate orders
- obtaining warranties
- avoiding shortages or running out of materials or supplies
- controlling inventory levels and keeping theft to minimum
- planning realistic lead times and expediting deliveries

- handling defective or damaged shipments and returning shipments
- using purchasing reports to spot "hidden" problems (For example, the vendor may be a low bidder, but the small print allows them to charge a "markup" price on supplies used or to charge their hourly rate from the moment they leave their office to the moment they check back into the office. These charges can significantly increase the price without it showing up-front.)
- negotiating prices

4.5   Grants

Although it is not our intent to include a grant writing course within this volume, the facility manager should be aware that there are many excellent resources available that can assist library personnel with grant writing for monies that can be applied for the building. While it is not often that grant funds are available for the daily management of the facility, there is generous support for major capital projects such as renovation and construction and for the purchase of major equipment.

The three main sources of grant money are government (federal, state, county, city), foundations, and corporations and businesses.

One begins the process of applying for grant money by making a list of the needs the library has and comparing them with a list of sources that might match the needs you identify. You must be clear on what you already are and do, and what you think your facility needs to be. Having an accurate needs assessment will help you develop a profile for your project. Then, you will be able to check this against the various available funding sources to see if there is a "match" for your project with some source of revenue.

Leveraging money—that is, using what you have committed to the project to attract additional monies—is another option that is appropriate to use, especially when there is a campaign to raise significant money for a project. The initial money may be some that the board or the city sets aside, and this is announced as the kickoff to the campaign.

Recognition, then, becomes an important part of the fund-raising effort. There are always some individuals who will want to remain anonymous, but more will want at least to be thanked. Corporations and businesses often want to have their name out in front of the community so they can be portrayed as a good neighbor. Naming a new wing or a room in honor of a large donor is an example. Smaller donations might be included on bricks in a pathway that is being built. This type of recognition does not have to be gaudy or tacky; a tasteful plaque may be in order. Whatever route you choose to take with a "naming opportunity" needs to have board consideration before the fund-raising efforts begin.

Grant money also brings along with it accountability. The library director, as the organization's head, is responsible for the dollars that have been granted or raised through a grant or giving program. It is a must that a written report be filed. This report documents all the expenditures for the project and indicates if there are any variances between original budget projections in the application and the actual expenses, and the reasons for the variances. The final report should always be tied in with the project's goals, summarizing how the money was expended and how the dollars led to the effectiveness of the project.

4.6   Requests for Proposals

A request for proposals is a formal, legal process through which the purchaser attempts to get prices from several vendors for the same products and services. The information contained therein is designed so that the purchaser will be able to compare "apples to apples" and then truly have a clear picture of what is the best price. This information is then put into the formal contract.

Figure 4–1 is a sample of a request for proposal for a telecommunications system.

4.7   Contracts

A contract is a legal agreement for a specific service or product. It is a document intended to protect both parties by spelling out what is required from each. In many cases, information from the bid documents or the request for proposals is included in the text of the contracts.

Standard forms of contracts are often used, especially in regard to construction or to any major work to buildings. A good source for a standard contract are the documents produced jointly by the National Society of Professional Engineers with the American Consulting Engineers, Professional Engineers in Private Practice, and the Construction Specifications Institute. The Associated General Contractors of America have also endorsed this contract. With assistance from your legal advisors, you should be able to use most of this contract as it is and make some adaptations to fit your specific situation.

Some of the areas that are included in a contract document are: the scope of the project; the estimate of time needed to complete it; payment procedures; specifics concerning materials to be used; insurance requirements; performance bonds; the need for and the type of permits; specifics from any local ordinance as a code of ethics; and affirmative action policy statements.

Figure 4–1
Request for Proposal (RFP)

Proprietary Notice

The transmission of this RFP to a prospective vendor or acceptance of a reply from a vendor shall not imply an obligation or commitment on the part of the City. Specifically, there will be no obligation to pay for proposal preparation work, pre-engineering work, or any obligation to enter into a contract or agreement.

General Instructions for Proposers

This Request for Proposal consists of several items outlined in the Table of Contents. Please review the package prior to its submission to ensure that all items are present. If any are missing, please call Ms. Purchaser of the City at 111–630–1234.

All sections of this RFP must be completed. The quality of the response to the RFP can only be viewed as an example of the vendor's capabilities. After each stipulation and/or paragraph, enter the word in **bold type** *"acknowledge"* or *"exception,"* indicating your compliance or noncompliance with the specification. An alternative and/or explanation is suggested after each "exception" explaining your noncompliance or alteration to the specification.

Only existing telephone equipment will be considered. Telephone equipment under development, in planning, or in beta test will not be considered.

Proposals are due no later than January 31, 2002 to:

> Purchasing Officer
> City
> Main St. Room 0001
> Anytown, USA 06450–8022
> 111–630–0052 (fax)

The proposed telephone equipment should be immediately demonstrable at existing customer locations.

All submitted proposals will be considered the property of the City.

To assist in the preparation of proposals, vendors will be given an opportunity to directly inspect the Municipality's sites on 1–20–02 at 9:00 a.m.

Separate pricing and contracts are required for both the Library and City Hall.

Figure 4–1
(Continued)

Table of Contents

Introduction

      Background and Objectives

      RFP Timeline

General Requirements for Proposers

      General Requirements

      Procedures and Schedules

      Clarification and Addenda

      Evaluation Criteria

      Project Award

      RFP Format and Issues

Proposal Specifications

Financial Information

Telephone Equipment Capabilities and Features

Vendor Company Information

Vendor Installation, Service, and Support Policies

Required Attachments

Additional Information

Acknowledgments

INTRODUCTION

Background and Objectives

The City has identified the following objectives:

To replace current telephone equipment, providing capacity and capability for current and future requirements;

      A 2Q *2000* installation completion and cutover is desired;

Figure 4–1
(*Continued*)

RFP Timeline

The following schedule of events will be used to complete the selection of the equipment and vendor:

Action Items	Responsibility	Date
1. Issue RFP to Vendor	*City*	1/12/2002
2. Delivery of Proposals	Vendor	1/31/2002
3. Evaluate Proposals Committee Review	*City*	2/15/2002
4. Vendor Selection & Contract Negotiations	*City & Vendor*	3/1/2002
5. Develop Implementation Plan	*City & Vendor*	3/1/2002
6. Installation/Cutover Complete	Vendor	TBD

GENERAL REQUIREMENTS FOR PROPOSERS

General Requirements

A vendor, by making the proposal, represents that the company possesses the capabilities, hardware and personnel necessary to provide an efficient and successful installation of a properly operating telephone system and ensures continued maintenance and support of the proposed telephone system.

All proposals should include all information solicited by the RFP plus any additional data, prints, and literature that the vendor deems pertinent to the understanding and evaluating of the proposal.

Any interpretations of, corrections, or changes to this RFP will be made by the addenda, which will be provided to all vendors. Interpretations, corrections, or changes made in any other manner will not be binding, and vendors shall not rely upon such interpretations, corrections, or changes.

Costs provided must reflect current pricing in effect.

The vendor is required to assist the City in staffing a Help Desk during cutover to answer station user's questions.

All RFP responses become a *contractual obligation* for both the vendor and the City.

Figure 4–1
(Continued)

Procedures and Schedules

This solicitation is for a proposal to provide telephone equipment to serve the City locations. It is the desire of the City that the equipment provided be able to support all present and planned applications.

Any telephone features not listed by the City in this solicitation, and which the proposer feels could be of benefit to the City, should be proposed with a full description of the advantages to the City.

Proposers must conform to the response format detailed at the end of this section.

This response format allows an objective evaluation of all proposals on a weighted matrix. Failure to comply with this format will result in rejection of the proposal.

All proposals submitted in response to this RFP become the property of the City of Anytown.

Receipt of proposals from the various proposers does not obligate the City. The right to accept or reject any or all proposals is reserved by the City.

Proposers shall insert all prices as indicated throughout the specification. PROPOSALS MUST BE FIRM. All pricing information shall be supplied according to procedures as defined in Financial Section 4.

The City reserves the right to determine whether a proposer has the ability and resources to perform the contract in full and comply with all specifications.

All pertinent technical information (e.g., brochures, system specifications, and operational descriptions) shall be included in the proposal.

Include copies of all applicable, proposed contracts in the response.

The submission of alternative methods of compliance to specific requirements is encouraged where any proposer cannot meet conformity with particular specifications. Note any inability to conform to a specific requirement.

Clarification and Addenda

Any proposer may withdraw or modify his proposal at any time prior to the scheduled closing time for receipt of proposals. *Note*: Only letters, facsimiles, or other written requests for modification or correction will be accepted. These modifications or corrections must be received in the same manner as the previously submitted proposals, and are only accepted by the City prior to the scheduled closing time for receipt of proposals.

Figure 4–1
(Continued)

The City reserves the right to amend or cancel the Request for Proposal at any time, for any reason.

Evaluation Criteria

Responses will be evaluated against the following criteria, listed in order of importance:

the quality and depth of the overall solution to the RFP specifications

ease of implementation, management, and operation of the proposed solution

proposer's experience with implementing and maintaining the proposed solution

total cost for the proposed solution, including estimated quantity and cost of ancillary equipment, plus impact on operational staff

ease of migrating to evolving technologies and services

proposer's financial status and strength, industry reputation, and commitment to evolving its product

Project Award

All proposers will be notified concerning the City decision.

The proposal that is accepted will be incorporated into a contract between the City and the selected vendor.

RFP Format and Issues

Please note that the RFP is divided into numbered sections. Proposers are required to comply with the RFP format, to utilize the forms provided for answers to specific questions, and to respond to all items requested. The first section presents a general overview of the equipment required. The overview should include the equipment configuration and required ancillary items and a description of how each item interfaces and operates with one another.

Proposal Presentation

The proposal should provide a straightforward, concise description of the vendor's abilities to satisfy the requirements of this proposal specification. Type responses in bold. After every requirement or stipulation, enter either "acknowledge" or "exception" to indicate compliance, noncompliance, or deviation from the requirement. Explanations on exceptions are encouraged.

Figure 4–1
(*Continued*)

Cost for Proposal Presentation

Costs for developing proposals are entirely the responsibility of the proposing vendor and shall not be chargeable in any manner to the City

Use of Proposals

The City reserves the right to use any and all concepts contained in proposals submitted in response to this RFP and any amendments. Selection or rejection of a proposal shall not affect this right.

News Release(s)

News releases(s) pertaining to this RFP or the award of any contract as a result of the proposal submitted by a vendor may not be made without the prior written consent of the City.

Installation

The cutover to the new system will occur in 2Q 2000.

License and Insurance

The selected contractor will obtain any necessary licenses or permits and provide evidence of insurance sufficient to indemnify the City from any and all claims brought as a result of the actions of the contractor, its agents, and employees. Such insurance should include, but not be limited to: worker's compensation, general liability, and a performance bond to guarantee completion under any contract.

Shipping, Handling, and Storage

The selected contractor will be responsible for the shipping, handling, and storage of all equipment and material to secure and protect it from theft.

Protection of Customer Property

All City property, including but not limited to office equipment and computers, shall be adequately protected from damage and debris by the selected installation and service entities.

Conformity with Codes

All installation work shall be done neatly, in a high quality manner, and in conformity with local and federal building and other codes.

Figure 4–1
(*Continued*)

New Equipment

All proposed equipment will be new. Included in this requirement: telephones, cable, connectors, and any and all apparatus used to complete the installation.

Prior Information

Any information that may have been released either orally or in writing prior to the issuance of this RFP shall be deemed preliminary in nature and bind neither the City nor the vendor.

Vendor Contract

The accepted proposal will be incorporated into the contract that the City will enter into with the vendor.

Proposed Cost

The vendor's minimum acceptable cost proposal should be quoted, as the City does not intend to negotiate the price after the vendor is selected.

Prime Contractor Responsibility

If the proposed services include the use of products or services of another company, the City will hold the vendor responsible for the proposed equipment as the prime contractor.

PROPOSAL SPECIFICATIONS

Equipment Configuration

Configuration: Equipped

City Hall

25   Digital sets, 2–line capability, speakerphone, 36 character display, message waiting lamp.

10   Digital, single-line phones, message waiting lamp.

Library

25   Digital sets, 2–line capability, speakerphone, 36 character display, message waiting lamp.

10   Digital, single-line phones, message waiting lamp.

Cabling as may be required if existing is nonusable.

Tone and test of all telephones, cable; warranty as new.

Figure 4–1
(*Continued*)

Configuration: Integration

All phones must be compatible with Central Link 3100 services.

All phones must integrate with the City current Voice Mail system—OCTEL VMX 200—to provide message waiting lamp.

It is anticipated that the majority of the labor will be performed during normal working hours. Due to the City environment, it may be necessary that portions of the cable work be performed outside the normal working hours.

Vendors are urged to collect sufficient information during the site survey to provide for special requirements in the proposal.

FINANCIAL INFORMATION

Purchase Costs

Total cost of proposed equipment, excluding tax, including all materials and labor.

Telephones and Cable _____

Leasing Alternative

The City is interested in evaluating lease programs offered by the proposer. The City reserves the right to procure its own financing based on the purchased price offered or toward the basis of the lease, whichever the City determines to be in its best interest.

Warranty and Maintenance

Telephone Equipment and Cable

Year 1 _____

Year 2 _____

Year 3 _____

Year 4 _____

Year 5 _____

Addition and Deletion Schedule

Price Per Unit of Equipment (Materials Only) Note: Pre-Cutover price must be valid from proposal date up to 10 days post cutover; Post Cutover price must be valid for one year from cutover date.

Figure 4–1
(*Continued*)

Item	Pre-Cutover	Post-Cutover
Multiline digital sets		
Single line sets		
Cable—per foot [list type]		
Connectors—[list needed]		
Other—[list needed]		

TELEPHONE EQUIPMENT CAPABILITIES AND FEATURES

Telephone Equipment Capabilities

All digital voice telephones will have the following capabilities:

>one button access to the most commonly used features (e.g., hold, transfer, forward, speed dialing, call pickup) programmable per station

>feature buttons that can be individually programmed for the user's specific applications

>built-in volume control to modify the conversation level

>visible message waiting indicator

>ring tone modification

>modular plug interface (RJ11)

>optional 2–way speakerphone capability

>integrated intercom capability

Telephone Equipment Features

All telephones will have the following minimum feature capability:

Hold

Place a call on hold at the user's extension and hang up.

Message Waiting

Provides visual and audible notification of a message.

Figure 4–1
(Continued)

Park

Station user is able to transfer a call to another extension and place the call on hold without ringing the telephone.

Station Speed Dial

User is able to program frequently called numbers into memory from his own phone.

Transfer

Enables the user to transfer a call to another station, an attendant, or the voice mail system.

VENDOR COMPANY INFORMATION

Installed Base

 # of proposed telephones in the service area   _____

 # of technicians servicing proposed equipment in area   _____

 # of service centers in area   _____

 $ amount of proposed system spare parts inventory   _____

 Guaranteed service response time: _____

 Date of company founding   __/__/__

 Where is proposed equipment manufactured?   _____

 Telephone # for repair requests   _____

Maintenance Costs

Present maintenance hourly rate for time/materials service?   _____

$ for moves/adds/changes?   _____

Travel time included?   _____

Maintenance Coverage

Maintenance coverage is required 8 hours a day, 5 days a week. The cost for this coverage must be included in your proposal (e.g., cost for new equipment and cost proposed for second year maintenance).

Figure 4–1
(*Continued*)

Maintenance Records

Vendor is required to maintain current records on all aspects of the proposed equipment on site, including cable records.

Maintenance Procedure

Provide detail for escalation list and expedite procedure to be followed in the event of a service problem. Specify trouble duration/levels of expedite.

State of Development for Proposed System

Advise the date of delivery of the first equipment of this type. Approximate # of equipment of this type installed in the US to date.

Manufacturer's Support

If the vendor is a distributor and not a manufacturer of the proposed equipment, include the necessary letters or documents from the manufacturers stating their obligation to supply parts, engineering support, and service for the specified equipment.

Disaster Recovery Plan

In the event any of the telephone equipment is destroyed or made inoperable as a result of a major disaster, the selected vendor will use all applicable resources to correct the incident with a minimum of delay. City to provide detail for the disaster avoidance/disaster recovery plan.

References

Provide 10 customer references, comparable in size, technology and configuration.

Customer Name & Address	Install # System	Date	Contact Phones	Name + #

Figure 4–1
(Continued)

VENDOR INSTALLATION, SERVICE, AND SUPPORT POLICIES

Equipment Planning and Design

The vendor is *required* to:

> provide documentation at completion of site surveys and station user reviews for customer approval

> integrate customer-provided station design information into the overall equipment detailed requirements

The City will provide the following:

> station design information and departmental coordinators and contacts

Installation

The proposed equipment and installation must provide a turnkey solution, including required cable. Vendor will provide detailed specification recommendations for cable. For each required station cable run, detail allocation of wire for voice, data, and spare.

Project Organization

The vendor will submit a proposed schedule of activities for the entire project. For each major component, include an estimate of the start and completion dates. Vendor must provide a detailed implementation plan, including an organization chart for the installation team, identifying job functions and number of individuals required.

Vendor is required to conduct project status meetings. Provide examples of project management documentation for the installation process. Detail how reasonable installation standards are met.

General Issues

Proposers are advised that the supplier is responsible for but not limited to:

> provide turnkey installation service with a smooth and orderly transition to the new equipment

> coordinate telecommunication connections and any demarcation equipment

> obtain permission before proceeding with any work that involves cutting into or through any part of the building structure

---

Figure 4–1
(*Continued*)

---

supply a single point of contact for the project, installation, and maintenance personnel with appropriate materials, tools, and test instruments to fully meet the intent of this document

perform system testing and proper connection of station equipment and auxiliary devices

The City will provide the vendor-specified equipment environment (e.g., AC power, cooling, space, lighting) and electrical power service in accordance with the vendor's Customer Site Planning Guide. Any nonstandard outlets required by the vendor must be identified in the proposal. Vendor will include a list of the type and desired location of all electrical power connections required to fully support the proposed equipment both during test/acceptance and in full operation.

In addition, the City will provide the following:

physical access to facilities for the installation team and subcontractors at all reasonable hours

adequate detailed drawings and floor plans of the buildings

information on station locations and "as is" cable and cable pair assignments

alterations and repairs to building if it is determined to be desirable for modifications or extensions of equipment or services for safe operations

access for station cabling and testing

prompt inspections when notified by the proposer that the equipment, or any part thereof, is ready for inspection

approval of station floor plans prior to the start of work

Cutover and Acceptance

Upon the completion of the installation, vendor will test the equipment for conformity with the RFP requirements. When all tests have been completed to the vendor's satisfaction, vendor will provide written notice to the City together with certification that all applicable standards and specifications have been met. Vendor will provide written notice of the date on which the equipment is to be placed into service ("cutover").

On the cutover date, if the equipment is operating according to all applicable standards and specifications, the City will sign an acknowledgment stating that cutover is complete. It is understood that the vendor's warranty begins with cutover.

Figure 4–1
(*Continued*)

SERVICE AND MAINTENANCE

Warranty

Include a description of the standard warranty contracts that apply to the proposed equipment.

Describe the warranty on peripheral hardware products, if different than proposed warranty.

Specify any additional maintenance or support services available during the warranty term. Include literature describing these services and their associated prices.

RESPONSE TARGETS

Major Outages

Vendor is required to respond to major outages during the coverage period within the following time frame (e.g., 4 hours). If alternative response targets are available, indicate and provide pricing.

Minor Outages

Vendor will respond to minor outages during the coverage period within the following time frame (e.g., 24 hours).

Definitions

Time elapsed between vendor notification and start of on-site will constitute a response. Emergencies affecting a widespread user base, e.g., 20% or more users, constitutes a major outage. All other outages are considered minor. If vendor has alternative definitions, indicate these and provide pricing.

Moves, Adds, and Changes (MAC)

Provide separate pricing for routine MAC work. If pricing is based on an hourly rate, indicate the hourly rate used.

FULL SERVICE VERSUS SELF-MAINTENANCE

Off Hours Support

Advise if support is available 24 hours a day, including holidays, and whether a toll-free number is provided for remote support or dispatch.

Included Services

Vendor will advise if the following services are included (under warranty or under a maintenance contract) at no additional charge:

Figure 4–1
(*Continued*)

preventive maintenance

all parts and labor

vendor contact to assist with ongoing City needs

track service performance history (and make it available to the Municipality)

include literature and service contracts describing the vendor's support services

Service Alternatives

Describe what, if any, service responsibilities the City may assume for a reduction in the service pricing. Vendor should indicate available services and associated charges.

SERVICE COMMITMENT

Support Organization

Outline the capabilities of the servicing organization. Vendor comments should include the number of local repair and operations personnel, their parts and distribution system, and any other areas that demonstrate the vendor's service commitment (e.g., customer testimonials or annual reports that document financial stability).

If subcontractors are used, provide their name, qualifications, and functions to be performed.

Training

Provide a training plan for station users and administrator(s). Indicate what training is included with the price of the system, additional training that is available after cutover, and respective charges. Include:

course abstract

length of each training class

number of participants per class

Training Requirements

The vendor selected agrees to provide:

training on the telephones prior to the cutover, as well as coverage the day of/day after cutover as needed

on cutover day, provide individual trainers for the station users

schedule review ("makeup") training sessions a week after cutover

Figure 4–1
(*Continued*)

provide a station user's manual for every installed telephone prior to cutover

on cutover day, provide telephone training and feature review to all station users

provide in-house training to designated individuals (train-the-trainer)

Training Class Length

Advise the estimated class length for:

single-line set

multiline set

REQUIRED ATTACHMENTS

Provide the following attachments for equipment and cable option proposed as applicable:

complete list of references, containing name of Municipality, location, customer contact, telephone number, and date of installation for equipment that is configured similarly to this

purchase Contract form

maintenance Contract form

manufacturer's warranty or support letter

vendor's Annual Report or financial statement

station user guides (per type of telephone instrument proposed)

detail of critical dates and time frames for telephone installation

ADDITIONAL INFORMATION

Provide any additional information describing any unique capabilities concerning your company or the products proposed that are not specified elsewhere in this RFP.

ACKNOWLEDGMENTS

Indicate your acknowledgment that the proposed equipment and other requirements comply in all respects to the specifications set forth in this RFP unless specifically indicated otherwise.

Figure 4–1
(Continued)

Vendor Company _____

Authorized Representative (e.g., Officer, Owner, Director)

Name: _____

Title: _____

Signature: _____

Date: _____

4.8 Insurance Issues

Insurance has become a major cost item in recent times. We include this information in a chapter on finances, because insurance is often a hidden cost that is not taken into consideration when planning projects, and it should be. If your library is part of a municipality, then chances are the library will be covered under the plan it holds. In the case of special events, you will probably need to work with the risk manager in order to determine if an additional liability rider is necessary. If your library is a private association, you should pay particular attention to the issues especially in regard to replacement for damages to the facility and for liability issues.

Many cities that are self-insured use the technique of risk management. Risk management is nothing more than a commonsense approach to handling the potential ways in which an organization could suffer losses. This includes losses caused by fire, theft, flood, earthquake, liability lawsuits, work-related injuries to employees, and similar events. It attempts to handle these "loss exposures" at the lowest possible cost to the library. The process involves the logical steps of identifying risk, analyzing them and then selecting the best method for handling the risks. The risk management team would also then monitor the results. A form for risk management is provided for you in Chapter 5 and can help in assessing situations. The primary goal is to have a practical process for ensuring that the library operation is not impaired by losses that would threaten its survival.

Insurance is the process of financing the library's losses. This is actually an income-smoothing device that would spread the financial consequences over a period of time. Depending upon the extent of the library's operations, vehicle insurance (cars, bookmobiles), general liability coverage (for alleged bodily injuries), workman's compensation, and property insurance may be needed by the library. These policies would protect the library from settlements associated with lawsuits brought by third parties who are injured on the premises or related to damage to the facility and the collection.

Deductibles are usually in place on many of the liability policies. This is an amount of money that is paid for by the insured at the time of a claim, and it can significantly reduce the premium for the coverage. These deductibles can range from $250 to thousands of dollars. Deductibles can be written on either a per claim or a per occurrence basis, with the per claim deductible providing the largest reduction of the premium.

Property insurance differs from liability insurance in that it is first-party coverage. The insurance company, the second party, pays the policyholder for losses and damages. In liability insurance, the insurance company pays the third party, not the policyholder. In many states, there is legislation that dictates the minimum amount of insurance that a property owner is able to carry, thus ensuring that there is enough money to cover the third-party claims.

Improper property coverage can result in catastrophic financial consequences. It is wise to have a broad range of property coverage since any possible savings from reduced coverage would not be enough to make up for the consequences of fires and other perils.

The most important key to establishing an effective loss control and safety program is commitment from upper management. Safety and loss control must come from the top down. While it is beyond the scope of this book to delve into the area of insurance in more detail, we cannot recommend strongly enough how important it is for the library director to be aware of the types and amounts of insurance that are in place and to recognize that the library's efforts in prevention could provide substantial premium savings in the long run.

5 Keeping Records and Managing Reports

5.1   About the Papers: A Central Recordkeeping System

As librarians, we recognize the value of keeping accurate records of information for research. Our skill needs to be employed in running our own operations as well. Having a paper trail that documents equipment purchases and warranties, service calls on particular items such as an elevator or phone system, and information on steps that have been taken as preventive or corrective actions is an important tool in the proper management of a facility.

While *regular* and *routine* are words that conjure up an image of boredom, they are the words that can be a blessing in a preventive maintenance program. The facts show that the life expectancy of equipment and systems will be increased if specific, routine tasks are performed in a timely fashion. There is evidence that there are fewer emergency disruptions when preventive steps have been taking place, and this, in turn, may save considerable money. A preventive maintenance program ensures that current operations are in working order, by making any necessary repairs and replacing worn-out parts. It is also about keeping up to date on systems and equipment and can be used for future planning. A good preventive maintenance plan is organized and thorough and is designed to cover all aspects of the facility, its equipment, furniture, and landscaping.

Some types of systems and equipment need more attention due to their nature and to the amount of use they get. Some procedures will be relatively simple and easy for staff members to complete. Others may require the assistance of certified experts in a particular area in order to make sure the systems are working or to guarantee a warranty. (For example, a roof with a 20–year warranty may require semiannual inspections by a certified roofing professional.)

Although it may seem overwhelming at first to think that everything has to be checked on a regular basis, in the long run you will develop a feeling of security and confidence in your maintenance program if an organized process is followed. The time and the dollars that are directed to this type of program are really an investment in the facility's future.

5.2 A Preventive Maintenance Program

Preventive maintenance is the systematic planning, scheduling of inspections at regular intervals, and on-time completion of needed cleaning, lubricating, repairing, and replacing of items so that breakdowns are avoided, the life of capital systems is prolonged, and overall, the program has lower costs. To be effective, and worth doing, all preventive maintenance must be cost justified.

Establishing a preventive maintenance program requires identification of the work to be done, the frequency or the amount of calendar time between successive repetitions of the work, and the schedule of when the jobs are to be done. The first decision that the library director will have to make is to determine the area on which to concentrate. We must be realistic and prioritize work. We must know that we cannot get everything accomplished at once. The area or areas that are selected should be critical to the overall maintenance of the building and may even need serious attention. For example, your library may have an elevator that breaks down every week. Start with why it breaks down and proceed from there. Is it used more often on a particular day? For what purpose? Your goal is to get some immediate results by having it work when you need it. Not only will this provide you with the beginning of a regular program to keep the elevator in good repair, but you will also have the gratitude of the staff and others who use it regularly.

Once you have the system in good working order, you need to define what preventive maintenance inspections are needed on a regular basis. This will allow you to detect any deterioration that might lead to unsafe conditions or cause machinery damage and downtime. The main objective of preventive inspections is to ensure the safety and availability of equipment by keeping it in working condition at a low cost. Once a routine is established, and there is documentation from the inspection, you begin to develop a "history," which will be useful in projecting future monies needed for repair or replacement.

Depending on the type of system or equipment, inspections may be done on a daily, weekly, monthly, or even longer time schedule. To establish the frequency at which the maintenance assignments should be done, the library director or facilities manager must review the condition of the equipment and look at the history that has been created through documentation. It is important that the staff who use the equipment regularly be consulted. Using the vendor's recommendations is a helpful technique, too. However, you must remember these are prepared for "typical" use; if your library's use is unusually light or heavy, they must be adjusted accordingly.

Some preventive maintenance work requires a scheduled shutdown of particular equipment. This may be necessary to replace a major system component or to perform a complete overhaul such as with heating and cooling units. It is much better if the staff and the public are aware of the dates when the shutdown will occur. This planning will make for smoother operations and can help schedule other major work when the library tends to be "less busy." This is a much better option than having unplanned emergencies.

If your library does not have a custodial or maintenance staff to whom these preventive maintenance assignments will be given, as director you will have to determine who will perform these particular responsibilities. It is important that you communicate to that person or vendor the importance of keeping clear records for planning purposes and, in the event they leave your organization, someone else must be able to pick up where they left off. It is also helpful if the scheduling is done on a specific day, for example, the first day of the month. This is a good way of double-checking whether a system has received its periodic check. If the schedule is not being met, your system will not be effective in accomplishing the goal of a safe, reliable operation.

It may be that the first schedule that is developed is not adequate to track the needs you have or reveals that you may not need to check on certain things as often. We recommend that you make adjustments to your plan. The plan is intended to work for you, and you collect the information that will point you in the direction of the solution. When this type of preventive system is in place, you begin to document equipment use, longevity, and reliability. As you view data over a period of time, you begin to see trends and the cost-saving possibilities. New equipment may be a part of the answer and having the documented records allows you to budget for it and to project potential savings that may then be realized. Furthermore, a preventive maintenance plan means you are controlling the equipment rather than having it control you!

Unless a preventive maintenance program is performed in a timely manner, you cannot expect to have a smooth, trouble-free operation. You will have equipment that will perform poorly or not at all. You may have to fight with it constantly to keep it running. The approach of waiting until a shutdown occurs and then performing emergency repairs is not a good one. Chances are these fast emergency repairs are little more than a "band-aid," as they seldom last and then repairs are repeated when the next failure occurs.

Along with the preventive program, it is also important to include a predictive component to maintenance plans so that specific repair needs can be taken care of at times that are most convenient for the library. With this type of approach, you replace uncertainty with predictability. You troubleshoot problems before they erupt, and plan on repairs or replacements before systems fail. In order for your library to "predict" when equipment might fail, there must be someone assigned to the operation of the particular system who is sensitive to how it works. It is important to keep in touch with the staff members who use the equipment regularly. They know how it reacts on the best days, and they will be able to detect even subtle changes that might indicate something disastrous will likely occur.

5.3   Determining the Priority of Maintenance Work

As with any type of building, there is always something that needs to be done to keep a library well maintained. Responding to requests for work to be completed should be prioritized according to urgency. Everyone will tell you that his need is the most urgent, so, as director you will need to make objective decisions based on what you see as urgency and the information that you have collected through the program. Setting the priorities is a way of scheduling time to get the work done. This must be in the perspective of what the overall needs of the library are. Special events and other programs must also be taken into account.

The following is a system that we recommend for setting priorities with maintenance work. *Emergencies*, when they might involve risk of personal injury or damage to property, should always be designated as a number one priority. On the next level are things that must be accomplished within the parameters of the *work shift*. An example of this might be a broken lock. How will staff secure the library at closing time if this lock is not repaired before their shift ends? At the third level of priority are things that should be accomplished within a *24–hour* period. This might be the replacement of a shutoff valve that you have on the "off" mode, but still need a basin underneath it to catch drips. Priority four is *scheduled work* and anything that can wait more than 24 hours. It includes all routine repairs, preventive maintenance work, and installation of new equipment and systems. It is important that these jobs are scheduled with a date. Using ASAP (as soon as possible) is not good enough, because soon everyone will use it and give all work to be done the same urgency level. Your planned system will fall apart. Priority systems work best when the primary consideration of each task to be completed is compared to all other tasks and then assigned a response time according to the necessity of having the work completed.

5.4   Skills Required for Tasks and Work Scheduling

Setting priorities may also have something to do with whether you have someone available on staff who is able to perform the particular maintenance function or whether you will need to call in a specialist. It may be that there is someone who can complete the task, but not in the timely fashion in which you need it done. Facilities management is a give-and-take process, and you will have to make some judgement calls about it. In any event, you should have a list of staff people annotated with all of the skills they have. A quick glance at this list will let you know immediately if there is any possibility of someone on the list who will be able to do the job or if you should schedule the work with a private contractor right away.

In developing a work schedule (see Figure 5-1), the facilities manager lists the work that needs to be done. This schedule will include the regular day-to-day tasks and any additional tasks that are assigned to staff or need to have a staff liaison with an outside individual. Additional tasks are taken from the priority list that has been developed. At the end of the day, the person who is supervising reviews what has been accomplished and then deals with the incomplete or new work that has been scheduled. A review of a log that records this information is an important tool for estimating the amount of time that is spent on specific tasks and what each task costs.

5.5   What You Should Know About Your Building

In order to keep up with daily maintenance issues and ahead of repairs, it is important to start with thorough knowledge of your building. Every facilities manager should know this from baseline information from a variety of sources, as well as by actually walking through and observing various aspects while the building is in operation.

Baseline information can be obtained through a variety of sources. These include the original bid specifications and the blueprints that were used for the construction of the building. Other sources are an equipment inventory and all the manuals that go along with the equipment; an outdoor landscaping list; a furnishing schedule; any consultant or inspection reports; and all contracts and warranties. A log of past repairs and service calls or past invoices might also indicate if there is some ongoing problem. Taking all of these together should give you a good snapshot of the facility.

As the facilities manager, you will want to perform regular building inspections that compare current conditions with these baselines in order to keep on top of repairs and develop a preventive maintenance schedule. Figure 5-2 is a list of the items that should be checked. You may need to adjust it somewhat for your particular building and geographic location.

Figure 5–1 Sample Work Schedule		
Date: **Supervisor:**		
	Daily Tasks Completed	**Preventive Tasks Completed**
Employee 1		
Employee 2		
Employee 3		
Employee 4		
Carried over to next day		

Figure 5–2
Inspection Checklist

Structure

Walls and foundation—What is their condition? Is there any cracking?

Floor—Does it feel solid? Are there any apparent cracks, creaks, and so on?

Stairs and railings—Are they firm?

Ceiling—Are there signs of moisture? Is it dirty around vents? Could the roof be leaking?

Water lines—Is there evidence of flooding in any area?

Exposed masonry—Is grout missing?

Are there any signs of wood rot or deterioration around windows and doors?

Is there any evidence of termites, powder pest beetles, and so on?

Electrical System

Is it adequate for the tasks being performed in all parts of the building?

Are there adequate outlets? Can the wiring handle the load capacity?

What is the condition of the circuit breakers or fuses?

Do lights flicker or dim?

Has there been any variation in the utility bills? Why?

Mechanical Systems

Heating and ventilating—Is equipment adequate to keep building at satisfactory temperature for all seasons? How old is the equipment? Is it too cool, too warm, drafty?

Is the insulation adequate?

Is there excessive noise?

Are any problems indicated by repetitive repairs?

Plumbing

Are toilet fixtures adequate for use?

Is there evidence of leaking pipes or fixtures?

Are there any broken or chipped surfaces?

Are the drains adequate or sluggish?

Figure 5–2
(Continued)

Is there enough hot water?

Is water pressure adequate?

Surface Coverings

Is paint peeled or cracked?

Would stain be better for exterior to reduce peeling?

Would siding be a better choice?

Is the hardware for doors, shutters, and windows in good operating condition?

Are metal rails and so forth rusty?

Is carpeting ripped or torn?

Are windows treatments in good repair?

5.6   Specific Areas to Consider During Inspections

Drainage

Soil that may be subject to water accumulations, especially with heavy rains or flash floods, should be well drained. Water must be kept away from the foundation of a building so it does not seep in and cause dampness. If water creates enough pressure against the structure of the building, severe cracking and other structural damage might occur.

Ceilings and Walls

After you are sure your roof is secure, you should then address any areas of the ceiling that may need attention. Depending on the type of ceiling you have, repainting and resurfacing may be all that is needed. In other instances, it may be necessary to replace ceiling tiles.

In the case of walls, if their surface is in good condition, much of their original brightness can be recaptured by simple washing with a detergent. Usually, the surface can be washed between eight and twelve times before repainting is necessary. This will be at a fraction of the cost of repainting. Walls should be washed from the bottom up to prevent streaking. However, if wall fixtures have been moved, or chips and other damage is present, it is probably time to paint the surface. The frequency of repainting will depend upon the amount of use and the condition.

There are times when both interior walls and exterior surfaces require special types of cleaning to remove graffiti. Special products should be used, depending on the type of wall surface. There are solvents such as lacquer thinner and acetone, paint strippers, abrasives, wire brushes, sandpaper, steel wool, and sealers that encapsulate the graffiti to prevent bleed-through. Removal of graffiti should be done as quickly as possible to discourage repeat offenders and to get it off the surface before it hardens and is much more difficult to remove.

Exterior Cleaning

Exterior cleaning is an ongoing process. Daily inspect and remove trash and other debris from entryways, stairs, walks, ramps, driveways, parking lots, and lawn. Stairs need to be swept on a regular basis; it might also be necessary to scrub or hose down stairs and walkways. Litter barrels and ashtrays should be placed at entrances for people to discard trash; these must be emptied daily. Glass and metal surfaces, especially in the entry areas, should be polished regularly. If the exterior walls are heavily soiled, an air-pressured, electric or gasoline-powered high-pressure washing might be in order. There are units that are suitable for washing brick, block, stone, wood, plastics, steel, and aluminum.

Windows and Doors

Commercial building windows and door treatments consist of steel, aluminum, or wood. Heating and cooling cost is reduced substantially when proper weather sealing material is applied around the frames. This includes caulking, weather stripping, insulation, and painting to seal caulking after it is set up. Door hardware often requires attention because doors open and shut so many times during the day. Over time, they may require some ongoing repair, including lubrication, adjustment, aligning, and weather sealing.

Resurfacing Facades

This is a technique used to update the appearance of older facilities and make them more appealing. Various methods can be utilized, including the addition of new siding, new brickwork, architectural hardware, shutters, doors, and windows.

Roof

The roof is a critical part of the integrity of the building structure. It provides weather protection and security to the rest of the building as well as to the contents beneath it. It may also support heating, ventilating, and air-conditioning equipment.

There are three major causes of damage to roofs: chemical attack (are chemicals being sprayed on trees and plants reaching the roof surface?), weather conditions (heat, radiation, snow, ice), and physical abuse.

A key to having a long-lasting roof is prompt identification of any problem and repair. A roof that is ignored will fail in one-half of its rated life. We recommend semiannual inspections to make sure the roof is in good condition, a recommendation that is often a part of warranty programs. A leaky roof can wreak havoc, costing much more than timely repair and maintenance. Look for signs of excessive wear and tear, including cracked or dried-up shingles; cracked caulk around vents, pipes, and valleys; worn or cracked metal flashing; and patches of mold and mildew. Gutters and leaders are crucial to roof drainage. If they are clogged, missing, or damaged, leaks and rotting may result. Repair or replace them immediately.

Of all of the structural issues we may inherit as library directors, problems with the roof are most common. They may also be the cause of significant damage to other parts of the facility and lead to damage to our collections. Because of the level of knowledge and expertise that is required to design a roof, we strongly recommend that the library director contract with an approved firm for architectural and engineering services when the roof is a problem. We also recommend this because of the number of reasons for a roof problem and the consequences if prompt attention is not given. The firm will have to consider the structural load-carrying capacity; the insulating value of the roof system; the presence of asbestos in the existing roof materials; the adequacy of the roof drainage system; and the overall general condition of the roof and related portions of the building structure. Depending on the architecture and age of your building, you may be asked to select a particular kind of roof for the replacement of the existing roof. Some of the roofing systems that are available include: built-up tar and gravel; metal; single-ply rubber; and asphalt shingles on wood trusses.

The following is an example of the appropriate steps that should be taken to determine if the existing roof should be repaired or replaced. It is a process that can be followed to gather information about replacement of other portions of the structure as well.

Figure 5–3
Roof Inspection Report

Area

Approximately 10,200 Square Feet

Condition

This is a large, smooth-surfaced, three-ply asphalt built-up roof over wood and corrugated steel roof deck. The roof is reportedly 15 years old. Over the years, leaking has occurred. This has been stopped by patches.

The roofing felts show normal weathering with the top coating wearing off, exposing the uncoated felts. These split and crack under normal movement causing the structure to leak. If leaking is allowed to continue, damage to the roof insulation will occur, necessitating a complete roof removal and replacement. Roof removal is not required at this time.

Scope of the work

The roof area is to be cleaned of all debris, old equipment, wood supports, dust, and dirt. All removed materials will be taken from the premises and will be properly disposed of by the roofing contractor. All heating, ventilating, and air-conditioning units will be lifted and the new roof membrane will be installed under them. Before the units are replaced, new wood sleeper and roof protection boards will be placed under each unit. All large blisters will be opened and drained and allowed to thoroughly dry. Felts will be heated and will be pressed together into the hot bitumen. Once the roof is clear and free of dust and dirt, the surface will be inspected for any deteriorated or exposed sections. Number 43 asphalt-saturated base felt will be installed over these and mechanically fastened to the roof deck. A bitumen roof system will be installed per the manufacturer's specifications, with lapped seams. The membrane will be installed with a complete band of continuity without voids to the clean, dry, smooth existing membrane.

All flashings are to be made with cut-modified bitumen flashing sheets, bedded in manufacturer-approved plastic cement. All pitch pots will be filled with approved plastic cement. Once the roof has cured, a manufacturer-approved aluminizer will be installed to the entire area. This coating is to be brushed at the rate of not less than one gallon per 150 square feet. Warranty to be provided will be based on manufacturer's material and labor.

Figure 5–4
Sample Specifications for a Roof Bid

The following is a sample of the type of information that is included in a bid proposal to repair or replace a roof. It, of course, will not apply to all roofs, but at least it will provide you with a sampling of what is appropriate to ask in a bid specification.

- The roof area is to be cleaned of all debris, old equipment, wood supports, dust, and dirt. All material that is removed must be taken from the premises and properly disposed of by the roofing contractor.

- All heating, ventilating, and air-conditioning units are to be lifted and the new roof membrane installed beneath all of the units. Before the units are replaced, new wood sleepers and roof protection boards are to be replaced under each unit.

- Any large blisters are to be opened, drained, and allowed to dry thoroughly. The felts are to be treated with seal ply torch melting the present bitumen. The felts are to be pressed into the hot bitumen and firmly pressed together.

- Once the roof is clear and free of dust, dirt, and debris, the surface must be inspected for any deterioration or exposed sections. Over these areas, there will be an appliction of #43 asphalt-saturated base felt or a manufacturer-approved equivalent, mechanically fastened to the roof deck.

- There will be an installation of GS Flintastic GTA, a nonwoven polyester mat-reinforced, APP 160 plasticized, modified bitumen roof system. This torch-applied system is to be installed per the manufacturer's specifications. All end seams are to be lapped a minimum of 6 inches and all side laps are to be 3 inches with 1-inch asphalt bleed out. The membrane is to be installed with a complete bond of continuity without voids to the clean, dry, and smooth existing membrane.

- All flashings are to be made with cut-modified bitumen flashing sheets. All top edges and outside edges of the bitumen are to be reinforced with a 4-inch glass membrane bedded in a manufacturer-approved plastic cement.

- All pitch pots are to be filled with manufacturer-approved cement.

- Once the roof has cured, there will be an installation of a manufacturer-approved fibrated roof aluminizer to the entire area. This coating is to be brush-applied at a rate of no less than 1 gallon per 150 square feet.

- Warranty: Provide a 12–year contractor and material manufacturer's guarantee against defects in both materials and labor. Warranty documentation is to be filed with the owner before payment is made.

- Payment: No payments will be made in advance. Payment will be made within 45 days of job completion and acceptance by the library board.

Figure 5–5
Sample Preventive Maintenance Schedule

Equipment/Area	Occurrence	Responsibility
Emergency Generator	Weekly	Facilities Manager
Vehicles	Weekly	Driver
Septic Pumps	Weekly	Facilities Manager
Heating/Hot Water	Weekly	Facilities Manager
Staff Lounge Kitchen	Weekly	Facilities Manager
Program Room Kitchen	Weekly	Facilities Manager
Electric Outlets/Light Fixtures	Weekly	Facilities Manager
Alarm System	Weekly	Security
Air Conditioner	Seasonally	Outside Vendor
Air-Handling Units	Thrice Yearly	Outside Vendor
Emergency Lights	Monthly	Security
Fire Extinguishers	Monthly	Security
Fire Alarm	Semiannually	Outside Vendor
Smoke Detector	Semiannually	Outside Vendor
Boilers	Semiannually	Outside Vendor
Fire Inspection	Annually	With Fire Department

Figure 5–6
Sample Building Observation Sheet

Use the following form to record information that is observed during a building inspection. You can then develop a plan to repair or replace as needed.

BUILDING OBSERVATION INSPECTION SHEET

Date:

Name:

Location	Condition Observed	Response/Action	Warning Signs

5.7   The Importance of a Central Recordkeeping System

As librarians, we know how important it is for bibliographic control to keep accurate, detailed records. The facilities management component of our operation is no different. Recordkeeping is essential for reasons of inspection, for warranties and guarantees, for liability issues, and in the preventive maintenance process. This documentation is proof that things were attended to in a timely and orderly fashion, and it may become valuable information under certain circumstances, such as risk management. In addition, recordkeeping is invaluable in assisting the facilities manager in the scheduling of repair or renovation activities, and it is an effective way to gather information for the budget process.

Keep track of requests for repairs, or other special attention that may need to be given to a particular area. This is important for the scheduling of repair and renovation. These records can be useful in predicting what long-range changes might be needed for various parts of the operation and in helping to plan work, especially when the requirements are out of the ordinary. Recordkeeping provides the documentation that preventive maintenance was done, often a requirement for warranties. Sample forms at the end of this chapter can assist you in organizing this work.

5.8   Information for Inventories

Keeping an inventory of equipment in and for the building is as essential to facilities management as it is to our collections. Inventories document ownership, which becomes important if you need to use the warranty or provide identifying information because of theft. To cite an example, a small microwave was taken from the kitchen that adjoins our public meeting room. From the window, a staff member saw a young man running down the street with it. A call to the local police sent them to the nearest pawn shop, which is only one street away. The police caught the offender as he was trying to pawn our microwave, and we were called to provide identification for it before we could get it back! Although we joked that we could identify it from the spaghetti sauce on the inside, what we really had to provide was make, model, and serial number. Because we had a file with this information recorded, we were able to retrieve our microwave. Although this was a small item, the same process applies to all equipment.

Keep the following information on file.

Property Identification

1. Brand Name
2. Product Description
3. Serial Number

 4. Model Number
 5. Condition (This needs to be updated at least twice a year.)
 6. Date Acquired
 7. Place Acquired
 8. Cost When New
 9. Warranties
 10. Individual or Department Assigned to

5.9 Record Retention Recommendations

Seven years
Accident and incident reports
Insurance claims
Vendor files
Leases

Ten years
Contracts
Legal agreements
Licenses
Warranties

Permanent
Blueprints
Drawings and specifications
Policy manuals
Bills of sale for major purchases

5.10 Records for the Bid Process

Getting bids on work to be done at a facility is standard procedure for most government agencies. This is to insure that the lowest price for the job has been negotiated and to protect against individuals who would simply award work to people they know, without regard to the price. In order for a bid to be fair, there must be a list of job specifications that is provided to each of the companies that want to submit a cost estimate. This way you are sure that each company is providing prices that are based on the exact same items, so that the cost comparisons will be fair.

The instructions in the bid documents should provide the standards by which the library will judge the materials. State any special preferences that are given to local companies over out-of-town contenders and considerations that are given to minority, women's, or disadvantaged business enterprises. The inclusion of the library's policy of nondiscrimination against any person because of race, color, religion, national origin, sex, sexual orientation, marital status, age, or disability in this information is important because it sends the message to the applicants that they will all be treated fairly. There should also be a reference to the fact that the library will comply with all applicable federal, state, and local laws, ordinances, and rules that govern equal employment opportunity.

A prebid conference is a way of explaining procedure and having potential bidders view the facility, if appropriate. This meeting is publicly announced and interested parties may attend. It gives the library director or facilities manager an opportunity to explain in detail any of the specific requirements contained in the bid document, and it gives the contractors an opportunity to ask questions, with all of the competitors hearing the answer. This ensures that everyone has the same information and protects the library from any charges of corruption in the bid practice.

In order to prepare a bid package, you must know what you need or how a project must be done and if there are alternative ways of doing it. You must be able to judge the bid packages and know when equal or comparable characteristics are present in equipment and materials. If you are not able to do so, you must get some assistance in making the awards.

A time-saver that can be employed in purchasing is to check whether your state has already gone through the bidding procedure for an item. It may have already checked with multiple suppliers and selected the lowest price. In many states, the contractor will honor the price and make it available to all municipalities, eliminating the necessity of going through the process yourself.

Materials to Include in Bid or Grant Applications

1. cover letter from administration regarding need
2. program description (what is the library's purpose)
3. prioritized requests based on urgency (This may allow the library to complete a project in phases if all of the funding is not in place.)
4. bid specifications
5. quotes and budget
6. workforce analysis
7. justifications for request (for instance, code violation)
8. letters of support
9. other documentation as needed

5.11 Purchasing Procedures

If the municipality has a purchasing policy in place, our recommendation is that the library follow it. If there is none in place, usually state purchasing departments have some policies and procedures that can be followed. There may be a dollar requirement; for instance, any purchase over $5,000 must go out to bid. However, in general, it should be a matter of standard practice to obtain estimates from more than one source so you can compare pricing, even if the item costs less than the recommended limit. Follow a standard checklist when soliciting estimates so you are sure all the vendors are giving you an estimate on the same specifications. Purchasing in some communities may be done by a third party, a central purchasing department. If this is the case, it is crucial that the library director and the facilities manager meet with this department about any specific considerations or needs that may be peculiar to the library. This will save a great deal of time and frustration later on.

The method of payment for a product or services is often covered in bids as well as contracts. This information may be important in the library's decision. You will need to know if the company winning the bid will require all of the money at the outset or whether other terms can be made available. In addition you might also want to have leasing options for equipment as well as purchasing options. The selection of a service provider may be influenced by the particular financial arrangements available.

While this bid or comparison of estimates process might seem time consuming, it is generally good practice because it protects the library for the long term.

5.12 Contractor's Liability Insurance

Most often, proof of insurance coverage is required of contractors when they are awarded a bid. Depending on the scope of the project, the minimum overage and the extent of coverage may be different. Areas of coverage may include a comprehensive general liability policy for bodily injury or death and property damage, worker's compensation and occupational diseases coverage as required by applicable laws, automobile liability, and products and hazardous operations coverage.

It is a good idea to have written into contacts that the contractor agrees to indemnify and hold harmless the library, the city, and employees from all lawsuits, claims, losses, and expenses, including court costs and attorneys' fees on account of any injury or death to any person that may be alleged to be in connection with the work covered by the particular contract.

5.13 Work Requests and Sample Forms

It is important to call upon all staff to report when something in their area of the library is in need of repair. This information must be brought to the attention of the library director or the facilities manager and, from experience, it is best when the information is presented in writing. There may have been times when you have been walking through the library on an errand and someone mentions there is an outlet not working. By the time you have completed the errand and returned to your desk, and probably have been stopped two or three other times, you may not remember what the first person told you! It is always better to put it in writing and put it into an appropriate place for retrieval. Use a "formal" form for this purpose, so that an indication can be made on it about the action that was taken and a copy sent back to the person who filed the request so he knows what is being done to correct the problem at hand. This also gives the director or designee the opportunity to consider if there is any other work in the facility that needs to be done by the same vendor or person. This, in the long run, can save time and money.

Emergency requests should be handled by the supervisor in change. There should be a list of numbers for all services and contracts available, and the supervisor will make the decision to call for assistance. If the situation is one where a repair is needed soon, but not immediately, the supervisor should leave a written request for the director so that action can be taken as soon as possible. If the emergency happens in the evening or on a weekend when the director is not in the building, and the supervisor feels that that the situation is urgent, a call should be made to the appropriate supplier or resource immediately. It is a wise director who has a plan in place and a list of helpers who can be called.

Figure 5–7
Sample Work Request Form

Work Request

Date

Date the request was initiated

Department

Name of the department that is reporting the need for repair/work

Identification of Area

Specific location of where the work needs to be done

Repair and Routine Work

Describe what repairs need to be made or suggest what preventive measures that might be taken that are not being done

Person Filing Report

Who is requesting the work

Date Received by Director:

Action Taken:

Date of Completion:

Date Returned to Sender:

Figure 5–8
Supervisor's Report Form

Supervisor's Report Form   **Date:**_____

Supervisor on Duty:_____

Facility:

Heat

Air Conditioning

Lighting

Plumbing

Parking Lot

Meeting Room(s)

Injuries

Complaints

Other

Figure 5–9
Risk Assessment Questionnaire

[   ] [   ] **Risk Code**

Name of Activity/Event:

Location of Activity/Event:

Start-up Date:_____   **Completion Date:**_____

Participating Parties:

Brief Description:

Responsible Department:

Contact Person/Telephone:

Form Prepared By: **Date:**

Key to Risk Codes

     01 Contracts, leases, agreements

     02 Assemblies, parades, celebrations

     03 Construction

     04 Operations, services, processes, programs

     05 Equipment, materials

     06 Special activities

     07 Other

Figure 5–10
Special Event Setup Request

Date Requested:

Name of the Event: _____

Location of the Event: _____

(What room is being used?)

Date of the Event: _____

Floor Plan:

(How should the room be set up? Are tables required? Is theater seating appropriate?)

Equipment Needed:

(List audiovisual equipment or anything else that should be set up.)

(The library should set a policy on the amount of notice that must be given for such a request. This is so that appropriate staffing can be scheduled.)

Figure 5–11
Checklist of Information to Be Included in Contracts and Agreements

Company Name

Company Address

Phone, Fax, E-mail

Vendor Number

Purchase Order Number

Nature of the Work to Be Performed

Description of Basic Purpose of the Document

Inspections

On-call

Repairs

Parts

Labor

Replacement of Worn Equipment

Exclusions

Payment Methods

Hours When Work Is to Be Performed

Requirements for Licenses/Permits

Replacements Due to Damage

Indemnification/Insurance

Termination/Breach of Agreement

Duration of Agreement

Circumstances Beyond Control That Prevent Performances

Applicability of Federal, State, and Local Laws

Date

Signatures

		Figure 5–12 Authorization For Equipment Repair Form		
Name of company doing repair	Address Phone	What equipment/ cost estimate	Date sent out	Approved/ Authorized by:

6 Designing Safety and Security Guidelines

Overview

Figures

6.1 Security and Safety Issues Overview

In a culture as violent as ours, it is inevitable that there will be incidents of violence, accidents, and security breaches within our workplace. While we cannot keep them out completely, we can watch for signs of potential danger and have a plan for intervention to halt a tragedy before it occurs. While security and safety concerns are an important part of the facilities manager's responsibility, every person in the organization should understand that each one must take an active role in preventing incidents. It is important to take the time to develop a process to deal with these issues to protect both the facility as an asset and the people who are in it. It is also important to audit the process on a somewhat regular basis to ensure that the library is in compliance with safety standards. As an administrator, you will also want to be able to control the access that visitors have to certain parts of your building without creating an unfriendly image to the public.

6.2 Dealing with Emergencies

While the administrative office has the responsibility of oversight of the facility, the cooperation of the staff is of utmost importance. The best way to cope with emergencies is to be sure staff members are prepared for various types of trouble and are familiar with the idiosyncrasies of the building. There should be supervisory staff on every shift who have this familiarity and are able to either deal with the issues themselves or notify the administration and appropriate community services.

Every staff member should be informed of general office safety procedures and should be expected to adhere to them. These include the obvious ones we all know (or should know) but about which we can become careless, such as leaving keys and purses in visible public spaces or forgetting to lock doors behind us when we are in a building alone. Staff should know who the appropriate security officials are and notify them whenever they observe anything that is out of the ordinary. This is especially true if there are suspicious persons or vehicles around after normal working hours. In the evening hours, staff should walk out to vehicles in groups with a security guard if available, and the security guard should wait until all have started their cars.

Staff should be extra alert and careful in all isolated spaces, especially in stairwells or elevators. Remind them to stand near the controls in elevators, so that an emergency button can be pushed in case of any incident. Every phone should have taped to it numbers for security, police, and fire, and the extensions of staff members who know CPR and first aid.

Simple tools that we use in our everyday office life have the potential of being used as weapons. These include scissors, paperweights, letter openers, and so forth. These should be kept out of the casual reach of all patrons.

There are areas, even in our public buildings, where the public should not be. Posting signs such as "Authorized Personnel Only" or "Staff Only" may be necessary for the overall safety and security of the staff and public alike. Having certain areas of the building accessible only with a key or with a keypad door lock is another solution for protection of the staff as well as the contents of the facility. A library is a great place to hide—our bookshelves, carrels, and stacks, as well as rest rooms, make this possible. Every staff member needs to proceed with caution, and these areas should be checked thoroughly before the building is secured at closing time.

State laws vary on the use of closed-circuit television for monitoring areas of buildings. It is best to check with local authorities before installing cameras, and ascertain the advisability of having signs posted that indicate that such devices are in use.

Staff should also have some sort of signaling system in place for various situations. Code words that can be announced over an intercom or to another staff member (for example, code "Adam" for a lost child), flashing lights, or even panic buttons may be appropriate tools that can be used to alert others to help. Unfortunately, today we can never be sure if a patron's behavior may become abusive or threatening, with or without a weapon. Signaling may seem extreme, but they can help reduce serious injury.

The library should also be armed with a security alarm for periods when it is closed. A telephone link to the company that monitors it and to the police department is a must. In most cases you will be asked to provide a prioritized list of those to be contacted in the event of a break-in or other emergency. There should be a limited number of people who know how to activate and deactivate this alarm. Otherwise, you run the risk of potential theft from unscrupulous employees.

All of these measures, when implemented together, will assist you in providing a more secure workplace.

Figure 6–1
Checklist of Emergency Guidelines

- The library must have an evacuation plan. All staff, but especially supervisors, should know the evacuation plan thoroughly. This plan includes knowing all the emergency exits and the location of fire alarms and fire extinguishers. It is critical that all staff and volunteers be accounted for. Having schedules in a convenient location helps with this. Due to the nature of our services, it is almost impossible to know what patrons are in our building at any given time. Sounding and flashing alarms, making announcements on the public address system, and having supervisory staff check their designated area of the building are other necessary steps that must be taken. The administrator or designee calls 911, and the supervisors direct all others to leave the building in a calm, orderly fashion. It is quite helpful if there is a predetermined area at which all staff will meet. Reentry to the building is allowed when approved by police or fire officials.

- The loss of electrical power can be from an external cause (as during a storm) or it may be from some interior failure. Supervisory staff should be aware of the location of circuit breakers and whom they should call if this adjustment does not work. Working flashlights (batteries checked frequently) should be kept in every department, and all staff members within that department must know where they are kept. While supervisors are checking for the cause of the problem, other staff members must know what to do with the equipment to prevent it from being damaged (unplugging it, for example).

- Supervisory staff need to know the location of the central control for the telephone unit, whether it will fail with loss of power, and who should be called if there are problems. If there is a loss of power, many phone systems will fail to operate. There should be at least one direct line or cell phone in the building that can be used to reach help. Everyone should know the location of several working cell phones.

- The company that monitors the library's security system and the local police and fire departments all keep an emergency file. The director's name and phone number as well as two or three other names and phone numbers should be provided.

- If there is flooding, the first step is to determine if it is due to water coming inside from an external problem, or if it is internal, because of a broken pipe or some other cause. If the problem is external, the appropriate notification must be given to the public works department or whoever handles this in your town. If it is an internal problem, the water valve should be shut off immediately. The supervisor organizes staff to prevent damage and loss of materials and equipment. Staff should be advised of

---

Figure 6–1
(Continued)

---

possible hazards, such as slippery floors, and the danger of using electrical equipment near water or while standing in water.

- A variety of problems may be the cause of unpleasant odors. The staff member in charge will need to determine if the odor is within the building, and from what source, or if it is an outside odor that is coming into the building through the air vents. Outdoor odors cannot be controlled, but there might be some decision to restrict the amount of outside air that is coming into the building. Internal problems that can cause odors include a gas leak, sewer gas, an electrical fire, or even a worn-out belt in the air-handling system. The supervisor will have to determine what it is and who should be called to deal with the problem. Depending upon the severity of the odor, evacuation may be in order.

- Vandalism is another area that may cause a building emergency. This usually involves some physical damage to the building itself. If a security guard is on staff, it is important that he and the supervisor in charge approach the suspect together and determine if the police should be called. Another staff member should be on standby to make the 911 call, especially if it is suspected that weapons of any kind may be involved. Whenever weapons are known to be present, an immediate 911 call and evacuation of the building are in order.

6.3   Putting Together a Comprehensive Safety Management Program

Librarians must be aware that a well organized, comprehensive safety program is beneficial to the success of their library. In addition, there is state and federal legislation that requires employers to pay close attention to the occupational health and safety of their employees and to involve their employees in executing these plans.

Efforts to improve safety practices need organized, goal-oriented accident prevention plans. For example, in Connecticut, joint management-labor safety committees promote safety awareness and cooperation between management and labor on related issues. It would be wise to establish such a committee in your library, even if it is not required by law. If you feel your library is too small to have such a committee, perhaps there is a department in your town that would like to work with you. Safety concerns are often similar and to have them brought out in the open and discussed is an important step in accident prevention.

A written policy statement on safe and healthy working conditions is crucial to make sure that everyone in the organization—including those who may be working off site—understand the priority that is being placed on safety and health protection. The library's program should be reviewed at least once a year so problems can be identified, conflicts resolved, and progress towards goals measured.

6.4 Occupational Safety and Health Administration Recommendations

OSHA (Occupational Safety and Health Administration) suggests five basic elements that are vital to a comprehensive safety management program. These include:

> *Management Commitment*: No program will be effective if the administration is not involved. A program needs direction from the top and supervisors and employees that take it seriously. Employees need to know that management regards the health and the safety of its workforce as important This is exhibited by the administrator being actively involved in safety issues; by communicating what steps are being taken to deal with particular safety issues; by encouraging employees to be involved in the operation of the safety program, having them identify and suggest corrections for hazards, and seriously implementing their suggestions; and by holding all employees accountable for shouldering their part of the responsibility for safety and health issues. The library director should address the library's position on security and safety at the employee's orientation session. Updates on this should be provided at all staff meetings, as well as reported to the board of directors.

> *Employee Involvement*: Who knows better than the employees themselves what kinds of problems and hazards will be encountered on the job. Employees provide valuable input on safety policies, safety committees, inspections, and in training. Realizing that workers are a key component in accident prevention, many organizations have tried a variety of incentive programs to keep employees focused on working safely. Whatever is used, the payoff to this type of program is that it does motivate. We encourage you to set up such a program in your library.

> *Safety Committees*: These are another way of promoting employee involvement. Safety committees generally develop and monitor the organization's policies. Tasks that the committee might do are: dis-

seminating safety policy materials; arranging for and conducting safety training; assessing safety equipment needs; and recommending appropriate safety programs based on assessed needs. In addition, these committees provide an opportunity for employees to use their technical and leadership skills, and perhaps develop new ones. It is a good idea to have representation from management as well as at least one member from each bargaining unit that has representation within the library. This committee has the responsibility of representing staff concerns and reporting back to the staff on what actions will be taken to rectify particular situations.

Work Site Analysis: Before an organization can design a new safety program or tune up an old one, it is important to know current status—how effective are existing procedures? The analysis should include: identification of hazards: regularity of safety and health inspections; reliability of the system for notifying management about hazards; investigation of accidents and near misses; and injury and illness trends. This analysis can be done by either walking around your facility and checking for what is and what is not being done or through a review of written records. Perhaps the best is a combination of both of these methods. We can also recommend bringing in an expert from outside the library. These paid professionals see your facility with fresh eyes and can spot situations you might miss because you are so accustomed to them.

Employee Training: Training is probably the primary means of communicating health and safety information to staff at all levels of the organization. Employee understanding is a key to accident prevention, and management needs to be sure that employees know what to expect and how they can protect themselves from harm by following the established health and safety rules. This training can be done under the oversight of the safety committee. There are terrific videos that are a real plus and can often be borrowed free of charge from local providers of insurance or even from police or fire departments. In addition, there are many companies that can be hired for training purposes.

6.5   Other Recommendations for Safety and Security

Accident Investigations: Investigation into what causes accidents is a primary tool available to us so we can prevent similar occurrences from happening again. The first priority whenever an accident occurs is, of course, to deal with the emergency. Then it is important to conduct an investigation as soon as possible after the accident takes place. This is because the facts about the accident are fresh in everyone's mind; because evidence at the accident scene will still be in place; and because witnesses will not have a chance to be influenced by others or forget what happened and how it happened. Photo documentation is a good way to preserve the evidence. Often, the insurance company will have guidelines to follow. They may even provide training workshops for staff.

Oftentimes, we bring in people to do repairs and they are unfamiliar with our building. Key safety issues need to be identified under the maintenance plan so that even outsiders are aware of precautions that your library has taken. Highlights can be posted in appropriate sites within your library. The following are some items that should be in a visible location in the event they become necessary.

First-Aid Kit: First-aid kits are available from a number of suppliers. Included are a variety of sizes of adhesive bandages, gauze pads, alcohol prep pads, antiseptic towelettes, ammonia inhalant, antibacterial ointment, and a thermal blanket. It is important to have kits in all areas of the building where staff can reach them easily and mounted on the walls of mechanical rooms so the contents are readily accessible. They should be checked and refilled on a regular schedule. It is important that a list of the nearby health services and ambulance services, with phone numbers and directions, are posted with first-aid kits to save time during an emergency.

Personal Safety and Personal Protective Equipment: While construction workers come prepared with their own, it is advisable to have some hard hats on site so you can observe work that is being done that might entail overhead or suspended construction. Safety glass with side shields or goggles are important even for such routine outside jobs as moving. Face masks are recommended when there is significant dust that may cause respiratory problems.

Fire Protection: One person and a backup should be assigned the responsibility for seeing that fire equipment is at full readiness and the procedures to control a possible fire at the library are being followed. This includes fire extinguishers that are in visible locations, and maintained by periodic inspection, and adequate emergency lighting. Any type of combustible material, including paint, should be stored in a metal fire-rated cabinet.

Temporary Heaters: It is not a good idea to have space heaters in confined areas such as a library, especially in public areas. However, if they become a must on a temporary basis, we recommend electric heaters, with the appropriate approvals, with proper guards, and grounded or double-insulated. Many states prohibit kerosene heaters; you will want to check your state regulations to see if this is true in your area.

Power Tools: Make sure electric power tools are grounded and that movable parts, such as gears and belts, are guarded. This includes something as simple as a paper cutter. It must have a guard to protect someone from cutting her fingers. Make sure that employees who are using this type of tool wear proper protective gear. Replace or repair a deficient tool immediately to prevent injury.

Ladders: Make sure that ladders are in good repair. Ladders with broken rungs, split rails, missing or broken feet, or other deficiencies should be repaired or replaced. Ladder side rails should extend at least 3 feet above the landings.

Stairways: All stairways must have railings on all exposed sides except the stairway entrance. They must be well lighted and clear of debris.

Figure 6–2
Comprehensive Safety Management Checklist

These checklists are by no means all-inclusive. You should add to them or delete items that do not apply to your library.

Employer Posting

- Is the required OSHA workplace poster displayed in a prominent location where all employees are likely to see it?

- Are emergency telephone numbers posted where they can be readily found in the case of an emergency?

- Have Material Safety Data Sheets been made readily available to those employees who may be exposed to chemical substances?

- Are signs like "exit," "room capacity," "exposure to microwave," and "elevator emergency" posted where appropriate?

Recordkeeping

- Are all occupational injuries or illnesses, except the minor ones that require only first aid, being recorded as required on the OSHA 200 log?

- Are employee medical records up to date and separate from personnel records?

- Have arrangements been made to keep records for the required legal period?

- Are operating permits and records up to date for such items as elevators?

- Are photocopies posted and originals kept on file.

Safety and Health Program

- Do you have an active safety and health program?

- Is one person clearly responsible for all activities in this program?

- Do you have a safety committee made up of management and labor representatives that meets regularly and reports in writing of its activities?

- Do you have a written procedure for handling in-house employee complaints regarding safety and health?

Medical Services and First Aid

- Is there a hospital or clinic for medical care in close proximity to your workplace?

- Are emergency phone numbers posted?

- Are first-aid kits accessible to each work area?

Figure 6–2
(*Continued*)

- Are first-aid kits periodically inspected and replenished as needed?

- If medical facilities are not near the workplace, is there at least one employee qualified to give first aid?

- Is anyone on the staff trained in CPR?

- Have you considered a defibrillator and are staff members qualified to use it?

Fire Protection

- Is the local fire department well acquainted with your library ?

- Is your fire alarm system tested annually?

- Are fire doors in good operating condition?

- Are portable fire extinguishers provided in adequate numbers and located in readily accessible places? Are they checked regularly for useable condition?

- Is there a regular fire drill procedure and evacuation plan in place?

- Are "No Smoking" signs posted in all locations where this applies?

- Do exit signs require batteries? Are they in good working order?

- Is there a sprinkler system? Is it tested annually?

Protective Clothing and Equipment

- Are protective gloves or other means provided to protect against cuts or corrosive chemicals?

- Are hard hats provided and worn where there is danger of falling objects?

- Is disposable protective clothing provided for cleanup of blood or other bodily fluids?

- Are disposable masks provided for work that may cause respiratory distress?

General Work Environment

- Are all work sites clean and orderly?

- Are surfaces kept dry or are they slip-resistant?

- Are spilled materials cleaned up immediately?

- Are there adequate toilet and washing facilities? Are they kept sanitary?

- Are work areas adequately illuminated?

Figure 6–2
(*Continued*)

Walkways, Floors, Walls, and Stairs

• Are aisles and passageways clear?

• Are holes in floors, sidewalks, or other walking surfaces repaired properly or covered until repairs can be made?

• Are guardrails provided wherever the walkway surface is elevated more than 30 inches above the ground?

• Is the glass in the windows, doors, and so on, of sufficient thickness and type for its use?

• Are standard rails used on all stairways with more than 4 stairs?

• Are stairs provided with a slip-resistant surface?

• Do handrails have at least $1\frac{1}{2}$ inches of clearance between them and the wall they are mounted on?

• Can rails withstand a load of 200 pounds?

• Is the vertical distance between stairway landings limited to 12 feet or less?

Exiting and Egress

• Are all exits marked with an exit sign and illuminated by a reliable light source?

• Is the word EXIT at least 5 inches high?

• Are directions to exits marked with visible signs?

• Are doors, passageways, and stairways that are neither exits nor access to exits clearly marked "Not An Exit"?

• Are all exits free of obstruction?

• Are there at least two means of egress from various locations in the building that can be used in the event of an emergency?

• Are precautions taken to protect employees during any construction activity?

• Are doors that are used for exits constructed so that the means of exit is obvious?

• Do exit doors open from the direction of exit travel without the use of a key or special effort?

• If panic hardware is installed, is the door able to open with 15 pounds of force or less?

Figure 6–2
(*Continued*)

Environmental Controls

- Are work areas properly illuminated?

- Are employees instructed in emergency procedures?

- Is the ventilation in the work area appropriate for the work being performed?

- Are rest rooms kept in sanitary condition?

- Is the lunchroom or cafeteria kept clean, with running water?

- Are employees instructed in the proper manner of lifting heavy objects?

- Is there a list of hazardous substances used in your workplace?

- Are hazardous materials identified with a warning sign?

- Is there a written hazardous materials policy, appropriate Material Safety Data Sheets, and employee training regarding such in place?

Electrical

- Are employees required to report as soon as practical any obvious hazard in connection with electric equipment, outlets, and so on?

- Do the extension cords in use have the proper grounding?

- Are all unused electrical openings covered with appropriate covers or plates?

Material Handling

- Are aisleways kept clear to allow unhindered passage?

- Are hand trucks and book trucks maintained in safe operating condition?

- Are delivery locations clearly marked and free from obstruction?

Transporting Materials

- Do all employees who operate library vehicles have valid driver's licenses?

- Are vehicles inspected and kept in good repair—lights, brakes, horns, mirrors, and so on?

- If the vehicle is transporting books, are they restrained in such a way so that they will not hurt an employee by falling during transportation?

Figure 6–3
Safety Committees

Various subcommittees can be formed under a central safety program in any organization. Depending on the size of your library and on the number of employees, you might break into subcommittees, or all the responsibility may fall onto a general safety committee. In some cases, the safety committee may be composed of members from other municipal departments as well as the library staff. This is usually very revealing as others from outside of the organization may see things with more clarity than those of us who are used to looking at the same things and people all the time. It is important that there are representatives from the administrative staff as well as from various bargaining units on the committee and that they meet regularly. A minimum standard of quarterly meetings is appropriate. In the interest of keeping everyone in the library informed about safety issues and concerns, each of the subcommittees should report out through the chair to all employees.

Physical Plant Safety Committee

This committee would oversee various plant safety issues, including security, utilities, and life safety. It would undertake a safety inspection of the facility at least once a year. This committee would also make sure there is proper monitoring for any hazardous substances and would oversee the orientation of new employees concerning the issues.

Accidents and Incidents Committee

This committee would review the reports for accidents or incidents that happened at the facility and determine if there was a connecting cause that could be corrected. The committee would be active in making sure changes happened so that a further accident could be avoided. This group would be responsible for educating employees on ways to prevent accidents. It is good policy to have this committee meet every time there is an accident that is significant or at least quarterly.

Health and Infection Control

Although risks from infections and blood-borne pathogens is usually not great in a library setting, it is important that the staff know how to deal with various situations. This includes the proper handling of "sharps" (needles and so forth) that may be found on the premises, bleeding cuts, or any situation where bodily waste is present. This committee would educate and monitor the staff on the proper techniques and precautions that are to be taken under the circumstances. It might also be in charge of educating the staff about proper techniques for lifting and for evaluating the ergonomics of various workstations. This committee would address the most common workplace injuries and what steps could be taken to prevent them.

Figure 6–4
Safety Committee Report

These types of items should be discussed during a safety committee meeting. Depending on the preference of the organization, bulleted notes such as these or notes in a more traditional format will serve as a record.

Physical Plant

- Reviewed and revised fire drill procedure and documentation to ensure proper procedures are in place and followed.

- Held fire drills quarterly.

- Developed and implemented a security audit and awareness program to identify risk-sensitive areas, evaluate existing security procedures, make recommendations to improve security, educate staff, and test staff security knowledge.

- Responded to safety issues reported by staff.

Accidents/Incidents

- Compared incidents with state and national rates for similar institutions.

- Revised and completed reporting forms; trained staff on completing them.

- New employee safety education training completed.

Emergency Preparedness

- Conducted staff training.

Figure 6–5
Potentially Difficult Behaviors and Management Techniques

Patrons exhibiting nervous-type activities, such as wringing their hands, can usually be quieted by a staff response that attempts to resolve the problem. Defensive, irrational, belligerent, or challenging behavior requires that the staff member respond by presenting clear choices with consequences attached in a firm, yet respectful manner. Different situations may call for different techniques. Sometimes, all the person wants to do is vent; attentive listening may be all that is required of the staff member. In other cases, it may be important to explain policy or procedures and how they apply to everyone.

The staff should attempt to avoid personal challenges, because they do not solve the problem and can actually exacerbate it. However, when a patron is physically violent, staff members should immediately implement the library's procedures, which must include calling for assistance. It is much better to get the situation under control immediately, rather than have staff or the public injured or killed because the offender was given choices.

All staff may not need to be trained on the same level. It really depends upon the amount of exposure they have with the public. However, key personnel responsible for security and safety must know all the risks and policies better than anyone else.

It is also a good idea to have a zero tolerance policy in place for *staff* members, so that everyone realizes that aggressive behavior will not be tolerated by *anyone.* It is quite possible that some of these behaviors may also be exhibited in staff members who are undergoing stressful situations or behavior changes. The actual management of the situation to protect the safety and security of all others within the facility may be exactly the same as if the person were from the "outside." However, other personnel policies may also be applied to deal with the employee. A sample of a zero tolerance policy follows.

Figure 6–6
Zero Tolerance Policy

Purpose of the Policy

To identify unacceptable behavior by employees that will not be tolerated by this library and to establish guidelines for dealing with employees who willingly and knowingly ignore this policy.

Policy

The library strongly disapproves of and will not tolerate threats, violent behavior, or acts of intimidation of any kind by an employee upon any other employee, visitor, or patron. All employees are forbidden to commit acts of offensive and inappropriate behavior in the work-place at any time whether on or off duty. Failure to comply will result in disciplinary action and possible termination.

It is every employee's responsibility to report all threats, acts of intimidation, harassment, violence (physical and verbal), and any other unacceptable behavior immediately to his supervisor. All reports will be investigated and recorded.

Examples of unacceptable behavior include but are not limited to the following:

> threatening phone calls or written messages
>
> vandalism of personal or company property
>
> following or stalking other employees or patrons
>
> assaults on other employees or their families
>
> threats of retaliation, getting even with management or other employees
>
> harassment in any form, verbal, written, or by gesture
>
> pushing, fighting, shoving, or horseplay
>
> carrying or displaying weapons of any kind, including but not limited to firearms, knives, martial arts weapons, bows, arrows, sling shots, blow darts, stun guns, and so forth

In some states carrying mace or pepper spray is also not tolerated. These regulations should always be posted.

Procedure

Please file complaint in writing to supervisor.

Figure 6–7
Workplace Violence Preparedness Checklist

These are recommended minimum requirements for any organization. You may want to establish others that are specific to your library.

- Provide first aid and comfort to victims.

- Notify law enforcement, emergency medical or fire department.

- Notify the manager, supervisors, and the board immediately.

- Secure the scene of the incident for law enforcement.

- Provide prompt reporting and briefing for other employees.

- Provide calm, reassuring staff to assist others in escaping the building.

- Notify victim's family. Be ready to offer immediate support and counseling.

- Know who to contact within your designated EAP (Employees Assistance Program) organization, and do so within 24 hours of the incident.

- Have designated library representative contact media with statement.

- Arrange for cleanup of site of incident after law enforcement releases it.

6.6   General Emergency Preparedness

Inspections are a way of the facility person showing responsibility for the building. It is recommended that these are done at least on a quarterly basis. Some equipment, such as fire extinguishers, should be inspected more frequently—we recommend at least once a month. Employees should become familiar with the location of these tools.

6.7   Maintaining Equipment for Safety

Regular checks on equipment used to maintain the building, as well as other equipment, are important ways of substantially reducing injuries and ensuring consistent, safe, and reliable service. Some of the items that require frequent checks, cleaning, and lubrication are chains and cables (for instance, on a garage door), electric outlets, power cords, switches, safety latches, grounding, and drive mechanisms. Further information about tools and equipment is also included in Chapter 9.

6.8   Safety Committees

As mentioned earlier, in keeping with OSHA guidelines, we recommend that the library have a safety committee. If the library is a medium to large library, that committee may be for the library only, with representatives from all labor unions involved as well as a representative from management. Small libraries may want to consider having this sort of committee with another department in the city or town or with an organization that has a similar mission (such as a museum). This gives the staff a broader perspective on some of the issues that may be of concern for both security and safety, and it gives the participants an opportunity to discuss and share ideas among themselves. In either case, it is important that the information is communicated to all employees. Therefore, we recommend a report that documents and shares the information. Figure 6-4 is an example of such a report and the type of information that should be communicated to all.

6.9   Defusing Difficult Situations

The library director must consider the role the facilities manager will play and what responsibilities will be assigned to him in situations that have a potential impact on the building through vandalism or some other form of destruction. Although there are entire volumes dedicated to dealing with problem patrons, and so forth, we felt it was necessary to include some helpful techniques in this book for defusing difficult situations.

Figure 6–8
Information for Inclusion in Incident Reports

WHO

Who was the perpetrator of the incident, and who else was present as a witness to the incident? This may become important later if there is a need to corroborate testimony where it's one person's word against another's.

WHAT

Exactly what happened? The "what" of the report includes all the facts and may also include your assessment of those facts. It will help if you are aware of which are facts and which are your assessments or opinions about the facts.

WHEN

When did the incident occur? If there were smaller events leading up to the main incident that is being described, when did these events occur?

WHERE

Where did this incident happen? In the building, on the first floor, in the parking lot? Be specific with the answer.

In many instances, difficulty with individuals may result in damage to the facility as well as interruption of library services. Therefore, we suggest that staff members should be aware that such situations do occur. Most often these situations are not caused by anything that the staff member or the library did to the patron. They may occur when a person's behavior suddenly changes and she becomes angry or even violent. It may be that a person enters the library who is not known to the staff and her behavior is inappropriate or even threatening to both staff and other patrons.

Have staff undergo training that can help them deal with these potentially difficult or out-of-control people. Employee Assistance Programs, the local hospital, and United Way organizations, among others, may be able to offer this training for your library free of charge or at reduced rates. The training should include ways for staff members to use their voice, body language, and personal space to relieve the tension of a situation and ways to set limits while remaining polite and respectful. The facilities management staff would get involved if there is the danger of the facility being vandalized in some way or to assist other staff as requested. Figure 6-5 lists some potentially difficult behaviors staff should be aware of.

Figure 6–9
Sample Equipment Requirements for Video Surveillance

Video Cameras, with auto iris, auto focus

(We recommend units with auto focus and auto iris that will automatically adjust to various light conditions. This will improve the ability of the camera to capture clear images.)

Digital Multiplexer

(This unit allows simultaneous recording on all cameras on premises; it should have zoom capability and playback functions.)

19-inch Color Monitor

(This size monitor provides an enlarged viewing screen. It will help you see details and the color capability may be important to collaborate with "eyewitness" accounts.)

Time-Lapse Recorder

(You will want at least 24 hours, but many are capable of up to 168 hours.)

There are warning signals that all workplaces must consider—from their patrons and from the employees. These include direct or veiled threats of harm; intimidation of others, both physical and verbal; and certainly carrying a concealed weapon or flashing a weapon to test others' reaction. It is recommended that the staff involved file an incident report that is kept on file with a supervisor. The supervisor or the library director will need to make a decision if the incident documented should be reported to the police.

The basic questions that journalists use provide a model of the information that should be included in an incident report (see Figure 6-8).

Although the director and other supervisory personnel will be involved in the crisis management of these situations, very often the issues may result in the need of the facilities management or maintenance staff to be involved. There may be windows to board up, glass to sweep up, or other building issues that will require immediate correction in order to secure the facility.

6.10   Video Surveillance Procedures

One of the ways to protect both materials and people is to have a system in place that monitors everyone coming and going in the building (see Figure 6-9). It is important to check the legality of having video surveillance cameras in your city and state and what other legal requirements must be met. These include posting notices that inform people that the surveillance is taking place. In order to be effective, there must be sufficient coverage with the cameras and the monitor that is used for viewing the images must be in a location that is staffed. Options are available so evidence can be recorded for authorities. The library director will make decisions regarding who will monitor the surveillance videos and how to handle the patrons or situations when inappropriate or illegal behavior is detected. Local police will be invaluable to the director and the staff in helping with the development of a procedure and policy and in training staff on effective and safe ways of approaching people who have been detected violating library policy and procedures or stealing.

There are companies that will prepare an audit and a proposal for the number of cameras to use within your facility. Many of them provide turnkey operations so that all the installation is done for you.

6.11 Insurance Issues

There is no question that there are insurance needs for any type of facility. These needs may vary, however, with the governance of the library. In some circumstances, the library may come under a general liability policy that the municipality has. In others, it may be necessary for the library to have its own plan. For everyday operations, a general liability policy is essential. This would cover personal injuries that might occur on the premises to either staff or patrons. If the library has any vehicles, either owned or leased, an automobile liability policy is also necessary. There will also, of course, be coverage to insure against loss of building, vehicles, and contents.

The issue of insurance is rather complex. Decisions will have to be made about the level of deductibles for the policies, as well as for the amount of insurance that should be in place. The library director will need to consider what the actual cash value of the property and its contents is and work with an insurance agent to determine the replacement costs that would be incurred if there were any problem. Additional insurance riders might need to be in place for coverage of special events, exhibits, and times of construction. The library director needs to require contractors to show their certificates of insurance as well.

There is also the issue of workmen's compensation and health insurance that the library, as an employer, must consider. Again, circumstances will dictate whether the library will have to have this type of coverage on its own or if the employees are covered under a general policy from the municipality. One recommendation that we can give for those libraries going solo is to check with the local chamber of commerce. Very often membership in a chamber will provide access to group benefits that an organization might not be eligible for in any other way, saving substantial money in the process. Further information about documentation that may be required for insurance purposes is covered in Chapter 5.

Figure 6–10
Insurance Checklist

Use the list below to assist in determining the areas that may need to be covered by an insurance policy.

Building Improvements

Any Leased Space

Furnishings

Fixtures

Equipment

Vehicles

Supplies

Materials (fine art, sculpture)

Property of Employees

Property of Patrons

Fire

Vandalism

Water Damage

Burglary or Theft

Earthquakes

Floods

Explosions

Premises

Operations

Employees

Personal Injury

Vehicles

Items on Loan from Other Libraries or Patrons (example: exhibit of artwork)

Figure 6–11
Sample Emergency Checklist

The following is a general emergency checklist that will alert you to areas that should be of concern to you as library director or facilities manager. These may not all be of concern to you or you may, in fact, have other areas of concern. This is an example of what you should do in your library to set up a checklist on how to react to problems.

What to Do in an Emergency

Problem	You will be alerted by	Do first	Do next	Other information
Fire	Pull call box or page "Code Red"	Evacuate all patrons	Supervisor calls 911	Use extinguisher if possible
Bomb threat	Call or patron	Signal co-worker to help monitor	Evacuate and call 911	Have security and law enforcement conduct search
Lost child	Crying, wandering	Page parent	Call for help if no response	Security to take charge until parent responds
Medical emergency	Patron or other staff	Make person comfortable	Call 911 and other staff for help	Remain calm; divert other patrons from area
Missing child	Concerned adult	Page child	Call law enforcement	Security/law enforcement searches
Power failure	No lights or power	Evacuate building and notify power company	Determine reason for loss	Stand by until building is determined safe
Security emergency	Patron or staff	Locate incident	Call 911	Keep other patrons away from incident

Figure 6–12
Emergency Telephone Number List

Director _____

Fire Department _____

Police Department _____

Ambulance _____

Fire Alarm Company _____

Security/Burglar Alarm Company _____

Security Personnel _____

Insurance Company _____

Glass/Window Company _____

Plumber _____

Electrician _____

Utility Company _____

Telephone Company _____

Elevator Repair _____

Exterminator _____

Janitorial Service _____

Locksmith _____

Legal Advisor _____

Public Works Department _____

Staff numbers might also be included on this list.

Figure 6–13
Safety and Security Checklist

Date checked:_____ **Conducted by:** _____

1. Are locks secure at all entrances/exits? _____ On offices?_____

2. Are emergency numbers posted at all public service areas? _____In staff lounge?

3. Is disaster manual located in an accessible place? _____

4. When was last inspection by Fire Department? _____

   Fire extinguishers available? _____ Last checked? _____

   Fire alarm tested recently? _____

   All smoke detectors operable? _____

   Public-address system operable? _____

   Emergency lighting operable where needed? _____

   First-aid kits available?_____

   Cellular phone service available? _____

5. Are all staff members familiar with the location of emergency equipment, flashlights, first-aid kits, shutoff valves for utilities? _____

6. When was the last fire drill?_____

7. Are exit lights in working order? _____

8. Are all chemicals properly stored? _____

9. Are any exits blocked? _____

10. Any indication of possible leaks? _____

11. Any worn or exposed wiring? _____

12. Any overloaded sockets? _____

13. Any ungrounded electrical equipment? _____

14. Any potentially unsafe condition? _____

7 Preparing Emergency and Disaster Plans

7.1 Fire and Disaster Preparedness

As we have mentioned in several places, it is much more effective to be prepared for emergencies before they happen, rather than just react to them when they occur. Therefore, we recommend that the library organize a plan that provides a course of action for all personnel to follow in emergency situations. It is the plan to follow should there be a fire, severe weather, or some other disaster that would affect the normal operation of the facility. The plan must be inclusive in its design so there will be alternative ways of emergency notification and egress. This is to accommodate any staff or visitor with a physical (usually visual or auditory) challenge. The plan should be practiced through scheduled drills so that appropriate adjustments can be made and the staff are not left with a course of action that will not work during emergency situations.

The objectives of the plan should be clearly stated. For example, statements similar to the following will serve as objectives:

1. provide safety to all of our clients, patrons, visitors, and personnel during such occurrence
2. provide a means for a safe and orderly evacuation process and emergency medical care if necessary

These regulations should conform to both federal and state regulations and the National Fire Protection Association's *NFPA 101, Life Safety Code.*

It is the responsibility of the library director to make sure all personnel and volunteer workers are informed of the policies and procedures that are to be used in case of an emergency. The most efficient way to do this is to begin the training during the library's orientation program for new employees and to continue it through routinely scheduled training and drills. In addition, the training should ensure that everyone reports a fire hazard or conditions that might create a fire hazard to the administration as soon as possible. The library director or the person responsible should investigate and make sure that such situations are corrected immediately. These include electrical, plumbing, or structural hazards.

The library director has the responsibility of informing the appropriate local authorities, such as the fire department, the police department, and civil defense units, of the established procedures. In fact, it is recommended that the library director meet with representatives of these organizations, review the plans, and ask for input. Members of these organizations have received special training to deal with emergencies of all types, and their expertise may be invaluable in helping formulate the library's plan.

If the library is governed by a board of directors, it is important that the director discuss with it the operational requirements for the library to remain functional. The board is the policy-setting arm of the operation, and if there is a need for a change from the ordinary, the board must empower the director with the authority to implement procedures so the library will be able to cope with the situation at hand. The library director, or her designee, must have the authority to expedite emergency procedures if conditions warrant them, without checking with the board. This includes closing earlier than scheduled times, delayed openings, or closing for a day or more.

The library director also has the responsibility to educate all personnel, including volunteer workers, student pages, and so on through an orientation program, training and fire drills. Drills are conducted to place emphasis on orderly and safe evacuation procedures and not just on how quickly an evacuation can be made.

The library director shall have the power to delegate some or all of the responsibility during an emergency if there is other trained staff able to act. A chain of command should be established ahead of time so there is no confusion about who is in charge during the emergency.

The board and the director should welcome suggestions and recommendations that would enhance the safety and well-being of all who use or work in the library. We recommend that these be submitted in writing and that a response be returned in writing from the board to the person making the suggestion.

7.2   The Need for Fire Drills

In order to have staff prepared to implement an emergency disaster plan, it is important that a series of drills be conducted to practice procedures. Drills are necessary to familiarize personnel with all the procedures and to establish these procedures as a matter of routine. Fire safety education has three major objectives The first is knowledge. We want to be sure that our staff have accurate, reliable information. The second is attitude. We want people to develop a strong sense of responsibility about fire safety for themselves and others. Finally, there is action. We want people to be able to practice and to perform actions that will enhance fire safety in their lives. This process will help alleviate some of the panic that can arise during emergency situations.

It is a good idea to have one fire drill per quarter per shift, one bomb threat drill per year per shift, two severe weather drills on each shift per year, and one general disaster drill annually for each shift. Have some drills that are announced and some that are not. Drills should also be conducted under varied conditions in order to simulate the unusual conditions that are caused by a disaster.

All staff within the facility at the time when the drill is being conducted must be required to fully participate in the drill and follow the instructions of the person in command. Staff should assist any patrons or other visitors within the facility and instruct them to follow the directions that are being issued for their own safety. The person in command can let everyone know that it is a "drill" and not the real thing; however, so there is no confusion, everyone must follow the instructions given.

The library director or facilities manager must keep a record in the administrative office of all the drills that have been conducted. These records should be available to all authorized personnel during the library's normal business hours for their inspection and review. The records must include the type of drill, the date and the time of the drill, the type of situation that was used, the type and location of alarm device employed (smoke or heat, pull station, and so on), number of staff and patrons participating in the drill, response time, analysis of the drill, name and signature of the person conducting the drill, and recommendations for improving the drill. The person conducting the drill should be responsible for completing the necessary documentation. He should put results on file in the library's administrative office with any backup materials within 48 hours of completion of the drill. It is recommended that this file be reviewed by the library's internal safety committee at least once a year. These records should be kept for a minimum of three years.

7.3   Procedures for Conducting Fire Drills

The library director, or the designated staff member, conducts these drills in accordance with established procedures. Notify the fire department and the alarm company that a drill will be conducted and that the library will be activating a specific alarm device. Once the alarm has been sounded, the person conducting the drill shall observe the actions of the staff to determine if established procedures were properly performed. After the completion of the drill, the alarm device that was used will be reset, and the report will be filed with the administrative office. Make arrangements to have the fire department participate in an exit drill at least once a year so that it can provide some feedback on the procedures that are being used.

In addition, it is recommended that "fire classes" be conducted for all staff on an annual basis, supplementing the scheduled fire drills. During the fire classes, staff should be reminded of the proper use of fire extinguishers, fire prevention tips, evacuation procedures, location of alarms and how to sound them, and any other issue that is deemed necessary by the administration. It is important to keep a record of the attendance at any training and have a list of what was covered on file.

7.4   Instructions for Fire Drills

- Know the sound of the fire alarm; it is serious.
- Stop whatever task you are doing; nothing is more important than life.
- Listen for directions from the supervisor; these may be critical for a safe evacuation.

- Proceed quickly to the nearest exit, directing patrons ahead of you. All staff should be aware of two means of egress since one may be blocked by smoke or fire.
- Move away from the building and go to the prearranged meeting place.
- Return to the building only when the fire commander or supervisor has indicated that it is safe.

7.5   Fire Alarm Systems

Some buildings have manual fire alarm pull stations that will automatically sound the fire alarm when activated. These should be strategically located throughout the building, and staff should know of these locations. Usually, the fire alarms are connected to a monitoring system that notifies the fire station when the alarm is activated. Heat and smoke detectors also automatically activate the fire alarm system when either smoke or intense heat is detected. A fire zone panel should be located near the main entrance of the library. When a fire occurs and automatically activates the fire alarm system, a light on the fire zone panel indicates the area of the building in which the fire is located. If the automatic fire alarm is sounded, staff should immediately check this panel to determine the area and take prompt action to evacuate that area.

The local fire department should have access to the master keys to the building if an emergency happens while the building is closed. These can be kept in a locked box on the outside of the building. The library staff should meet with the fire unit that would be the first to respond in case of an emergency so the unit can be familiar with the location of the key box and with the fire panel as well.

The library should be equipped with automatic, audible fire alarm signals, which when activated will sound a continuous, loud, ringing sound until the fire alarm system has been turned off. This will also sound an alarm at the monitoring company and will trigger the fire alarm panel to display zoning information, so emergency response can better pinpoint the area where there is a problem. A visual alarm system to assist anyone who is hearing impaired should also be employed. This can be located above each of the fire alarm bells and should activate simultaneously with the audible alarm. A blinking red light will indicate that a drill or actual emergency is in progress so individuals who might have difficulty hearing the alarm know when the facility is having a fire drill or when an actual emergency exists.

A procedure should be in place if the fire alarm system fails. This can be done over an intercom system or by communication of staff members to one another and to the public. A calm, even tone from the person delivering the message should be employed. Instead of just "Fire," use a statement like, "There is a fire emergency in the _____ (name the location). Please leave the building at the exit nearest you." This will help control the panic that could arise in such an emergency.

A posted schedule of all the staff members and all regular volunteers for a given week is critical. This is to ensure that a count can be taken once the evacuation has occured. In emergency circumstances, this will assist the person in control, who will need to take this with her, and other emergency rescuers to determine if there is anyone who is not accounted for, and therefore could still be in the facility.

7.6   The Importance of Floor Plans

In public buildings like libraries where there are several places people might go to find information, it is important that a floor plan be posted. The staff should review this plan from time to time so they are sure they are familiar with all means of egress. The public can also take notice of this if the plan is posted. The floor plan must list all the exits, primary and secondary evacuation routes, assembly areas, fire alarm pull stations, fire extinguishers, and any other data pertinent to the safety and well-being of all who use the building . These plans should be posted in the main lobby, on bulletin boards, at every supervisor's desk, in the administrative office area, in staff lounges, and in program and assembly rooms.

7.7   Fire and Smoke Barrier Doors

The library should be equipped with automatic fire and smoke barrier doors so a safer environment may be provided during an actual emergency. These doors must be closed at all times, and they should never be blocked. They should have signs that read "Fire Exit—Keep Door Closed" that are visible only in the direction of exit travel.

These are important safety features that can help contain fire and smoke from spreading. The local fire marshal's office will be able to provide you with vendors of doors that meet fire-rated standards.

7.8   Emergency Telephone Numbers

An emergency call roster is an important tool to have available for staff so that they will be able to notify appropriate library supervisors if there is a need to do so.

In addition to the city's emergency services (police and fire departments), as well as the alarm company, all staff members should have a list of who is to be called, with addresses and phone numbers, for use during emergency or disaster situations. The administrative office should have a listing of next-of-kin so they can be notified if the necessity arises. The information on these lists should be understood to be confidential and should not be given to anyone else for any purpose other than these emergency situations.

A listing of emergency medical assistance including hospitals, physicians, ambulances, and so on, should also be developed for use in an emergency or disaster. This listing should include the name of individuals to be contacted, their institution, and their telephone number. In addition to the regular staff, it is a good idea to have a listing of other support personnel that can be called in case of emergency. This includes civil defense, rescue squads, utility companies, and so forth that might be deemed necessary in an emergency situation.

It is important that every supervisor have this information and that it be kept in a location that can be readily found if the situation warrants it. As we know, information like this can become out of date rather easily. Verify information quarterly, and see that the updated lists are provided to anyone in the organization who needs one. The library director should assign this task to an individual who will verify the numbers, correct the rosters, and distribute them.

7.9   Emergency Communications and Staff Procedures

The library should have clearly established communications procedures in place in case a fire or other disaster should occur within the building or on the premises that could affect the safety and the well-being of any person. One never knows what damage will occur to systems, so there should be alternative plans in place as well. For instance, the library may want to depend on its public-address system. However, if the fire or disaster occurs in the area of the building where this equipment is located, it may not be possible to use it. Having phone extension lists, portable megaphones, or even walkie-talkies and cell phones available may be part of an alternate plan.

It is also wise to have some sort of set codes so the staff can be adequately notified without alarming the public. Examples might be "Code Red" for fire or "Code Black" for loss of power. These must be decided upon before the emergency happens, and every staff member must be aware of what they are.

Should it become necessary to evacuate the building, or any part of it, the staff should follow the posted evacuation routes and procedures. Familiarity with these is obtained only through repeated drills; we encourage you to have them quarterly.

Each of the rooms in the library, as well as the building itself, must be equipped with a minimum of two exits in order to be in code compliance. These should be remote from each other and should be clearly indicated by illuminated signs as well as shown on all evacuation plans. All exit areas should always remain clear and never blocked, even for a few minutes. Exits are a means of escape, and keeping them unobstructed at all times could mean the difference between life and death.

In an emergency, some decisions will have to be made concerning staffing patterns. In some instances, it may be important to call in some members of the staff who are currently off duty. In other instances, it would be wiser to send staff home and to make sure those who are off duty do not come in. The director must be prepared to evaluate these situations and to communicate messages through the supervisors about these procedures.

In cases of extreme emergency, the director will not be the person who makes the call. It may be a fire marshal, police official, or some other individual who has this responsibility. If a building has actually been evacuated, there may be need for a code or signal to return. This could be the standard "All Clear," or a "Code Green." In any event, people should not return to the library until this signal has been given. This will be after an inspection has been made by the fire department and it declares the area is safe.

If there is damage to the facility that might prove to be hazardous, the facilities manager and the library director will then need to implement an alternative plan. If preparations have been made in advance, other locations or materials and staff have been planned for. If not, individuals and materials will have to be relocated and reassigned until repairs can be made to damaged areas. In extreme cases, there may be a need to relocate to another facility entirely.

As part of the overall disaster plan, the person in command should notify the local hospital as well as the fire and the police departments of the number of injuries and the kinds of injuries so they can be prepared. If the fortunate thing happens, and there are no injuries, the hospital should then be notified that none have occurred.

7.10 Hazardous Areas

Hazardous areas, such as power rooms, boiler rooms, or flammable liquid storage areas should be so designated. These areas should be restricted to personnel who have reason to be there. During times of emergency, especially, only authorized personnel or the fire department should access these areas.

7.11 Incident Reports

When there is an incident of any kind that results in injury or loss of property, a report must be filed. We recommend that it be filled out within 24 hours of such an incident. This should be completed by the staff member who has had the problem or, if it was a member of the public, by the supervisor who was in charge at the time it happened. This report must include all the information relating to the event. Anyone who should be notified (risk manager, insurance company, appropriate state agency, and so on) should receive a copy of the report. There is further information about the need for this process in Chapters 5 and 6.

Figures 7-1 and 7-2 are examples of forms that can be used to assess risk and to report incidents.

7.12 Treating Injuries

If there is someone on staff who is qualified to treat injuries (is certified in CPR or first aid), he should do so if he is able. If not, the supervisor should call 911 or arrange for transportation to the closest hospital so treatment can be given. Personnel who are not qualified to provide emergency treatment should not do so.

The library director or the facilities manager should check on the injured party to make sure there has been follow-up to the injury and all appropriate parties (risk manager, insurance company) are informed of the progress.

**Figure: 7–1
Incident Report**

General Loss Information

Department_____Contact_____Telephone _____

Date of Loss_____Time_____Location _____

Description of Loss/Accident

_____

(Attach police, fire, OSHA, or other documents if appropriate)

Library Vehicle Loss Information

Year, Make, Model _____

Vehicle Identification Number _____

Driver's Name and Address_____

Driver's Date of Birth_____

Purpose of Vehicle Use _____

Describe Damage _____

Estimated Dollar Amount of Loss _____

Property Loss Information

Describe Property Loss

_____

Estimated Dollar Loss_____

Nonlibrary Property Loss Information

Describe Loss (Be Specific)_____

_____

Owner's Name and Address _____

Telephone_____Estimated Dollar Loss _____

Nonemployee Injury

Name and Address of Injured _____

Age_____Sex_____Extent of Injury _____

Treatment Given _____

Additional Comments _____

Date of Report_____Name of Reporter _____

Signature of Reporter _____

Figure 7–2
Risk Assessment Questionnaire

[ ] [ ] RISK CODE

Name of Activity or Event:

Location of Activity or Event:

Start-up Date and Completion Date:

Participating Parties:

Brief Description:

Safety Controls:

Responsible Department or Division: Contact Person and Telephone:

Prepared by:

_____

Signature

_____

Department/Division

Key to Risk Codes

01 Contracts, leases, agreements

02 Assemblies, parades, celebrations

03 Construction

04 Operations, services, processes, programs

05 Equipment, material

06 Special activities

07 Other

Figure 7–3
Fire, Safety, and Disaster Preparedness Operational Plans
and General Policies Procedures

1. Purpose

   The primary purpose of our Fire, Safety, and Disaster Preparedness Plans is to provide a clear course of action for all personnel to follow should a fire, severe weather, or other disaster occur that would affect the normal operation of our facility.

2. Applicability

   Our Fire, Safety, and Disaster Preparedness Plans shall apply equally to all persons without regard to race, color, creed, national origin, age, sex, religion, or handicap.

3. Objectives

   The objectives of our Fire, Safety, and Disaster Preparedness Plans are to:

   a. provide safety to our patrons and personnel during such occurrence

   b. provide a means for a safe and orderly evacuation process, emergency medical care, housing, and so on

   c. to establish our emergency plans as a matter of routine

4. Responsibility

   a. It shall be the responsibility of the Director of the Library to ensure that all personnel, patrons, volunteer workers, and appropriate local authorities are informed of the policies and the procedures outlined within this manual and the responsibility each has in following the established procedures.

   b. All personnel, including volunteer workers, students, and others, shall be informed of our established plans through a timely orientation program and routinely scheduled training and fire exit drill classes.

   c. Copies of this plan have been provided to the following local authorities: Police and Fire Departments and Civil Defense.

   d. A copy of all changes to this plan will be forwarded to these agencies within fourteen (14) days after such changes have been made.

5. Adoption of Policies

   The Board of Directors, through the Director of the Library, as well as other necessary support agencies and personnel, have adopted the Disaster Preparedness Plans outlined within this manual as those that best reflect the operational needs and requirements of the library to function during an emergency or disaster.

Figure 7–3
(*Continued*)

---

6. Delegation of Authority

   a. The Library Director shall have the power to delegate the authority of implementing these policies and procedures, or any part thereof, to other responsible persons.

   b. Should the Director elect to delegate such authority, it shall be in writing, signed, and dated, by both parties, unless emergency conditions warrant verbal delegation necessary to expedite these procedures, and such delegation shall remain in effect until it has been revoked or declined, or employment has been terminated.

7. Change in Policy

   a. We welcome any suggestions or recommendations that would enhance the safety and well-being of all concerned.

   b. All suggestions or recommendations shall be dated and submitted to the administration for review and disposition.

   c. It is recommended that all suggestions or recommendations be submitted in writing and signed by the person making such request.

   d. All suggestions or recommendations that request a written record of the administration's or committee's decision must be signed and dated by the person making such request.

   e. All suggestions or recommendations, except those authorized verbally during emergency conditions, shall be reviewed by the Safety Risk Committee, at its next regularly scheduled meeting, or sooner if deemed appropriate or necessary by the Director.

   f. Persons submitting a request for written decisions shall be notified of such decisions within ten (10) working days after the Safety Risk Committee's meeting.

8. Orientation

   a. All personnel, including volunteers and student workers, as well as others that may be appropriate, shall be required to undergo an orientation of this plan within the first two working days of employment or work assignment.

   b. Records shall be maintained to reflect the actual dates such individuals began and completed this orientation process.

Figure 7–3
(Continued)

---

9. Governing Regulations

    a. Regulations mandating the enclosed Fire, Safety, and Disaster Preparedness Plans are derived from current federal and state regulations and the National Fire Protection Association's *NFPA 101, Life Safety Code.*

    b. *The NFPA 101, Life Safety Code* is available upon request.

10. Chain of Command

    a. The chain of command, as established by the Board of Directors, shall be followed by all personnel at all times.

    b. The person in charge at the time a disaster or emergency occurs shall remain in charge until someone higher up in the chain of command arrives and relieves her or until local authorities having jurisdiction over such matters arrive and take command of the situation.

    c. Chain of Command: Director, Assistant Director, Department Supervisors.

11. Recordkeeping Requirements

    a. Emergency recordkeeping requirements will be implemented when such action becomes necessary.

    b. Records that will be maintained during emergency or disaster conditions are outlined throughout this plan.

12. Release of Information

    a. The Library Director or the person who is in charge at the time that an emergency or disaster occurs shall be the only person authorized to release information.

    b. All information shall be regarded as confidential and released to authorized personnel only.

    c. Authorized personnel shall include, but not necessarily be limited to: staff members, immediate family members, law enforcement agencies, health department officials, medical and support personnel, and city and state officials.

Figure 7–3
(*Continued*)

---

13. Drills

   a. The following drills shall be conducted to assist in preparing for emergency or disaster situations:

   fire drills—quarterly

   bomb threat drills—yearly

   tornado and severe weather—two per year

   disaster—yearly

   b. Drills are necessary and shall be conducted to familiarize all personnel with procedures and to establish them as a matter of routine.

   c. Drills may or may not be preannounced.

   d. Drills shall be conducted under varied conditions to simulate the usual conditions caused by a disaster.

   e. Drills are conducted to place emphasis on orderly and safe evacuation procedures rather than on how quickly evacuations can be made.

   f. All personnel within the facility at the time a drill is conducted shall be required to participate in the drill and follow all instructions issued.

   g. Patrons and visitors shall be directed by staff and will follow the directions and lead of the staff members.

   h. Smoking shall be prohibited during drills, even outside the library facility.

14. Record of Drills

   a. A record of all drills conducted shall be maintained in the administrative office and shall be made available to authorized persons during normal business hours for their inspection and review.

   b. A record of each drill conducted shall include, but not necessarily be limited to: the type of drill; the date and the time; a list of personnel participating; type of situation; location of the situation used; type of alarm device used (smoke or heat detector, pull station, and so on); location of the alarm device used; number of patrons and staff participating in the drill; response of the personnel; response time; analysis of the drill; name and signature of the person conducting the drill; recommendations for improvement of drills.

Figure 7–3
(*Continued*)

c. The person conducting the drill shall be responsible for completing the necessary documentation, unless otherwise directed, and such reports shall be submitted to the administration, along with any documentation that may be required to complete the necessary reports, within forty-eight (48) hours of the completion of the drill.

d. A record of all drills shall be reviewed by the Safety Risk Committee at least annually, and a written analysis shall be filed and maintained with such reports.

e. The record of drills shall be filed and maintained for a minimum of three (3) years, or until other lawful disposition has been made.

15. Conducting Drills

a. Fire Exit Drills:

(1) The Director or his designee shall be responsible for conducting the fire exit drill in accordance with the established procedure.

(2) A fire alarm pull station or the activation of a smoke or heat detector shall be selected for use prior to the drill.

(3) Once the selection has been made, the Fire Department and the Alarm Company shall be notified that a drill is being conducted and they will be notified when the drill is complete.

(4) Once the notifications have been made, the person conducting the drill shall proceed to the selected area and activate the alarm device.

(5) Once the alarm has sounded, the person conducting the drill shall observe the actions performed by individuals participating in the drill to establish if procedures are properly performed.

(6) After the completion of the drill, the alarm device activated shall be reset.

(7) The person conducting the drill shall contact the Fire Department and the Alarm Company and inform them that the drill has been conducted and ascertain whether or not the alarm was activated at the fire monitoring company. The results shall be noted in the Record of Drills.

Figure 7–3
(Continued)

---

(8)   The person conducting the drill shall be responsible for completing the Record of Drills report form and submitting it to administration as outlined in paragraph 14.

(9)   The Fire Department shall participate in fire exit drills annually.

b.   Miscellaneous Drills

(1)   Other disaster drills shall be conducted as outlined in paragraph 13

(2)   All drills conducted shall be recorded in the Record of Drills.

16.   In-Service Training

a.   In-service training classes shall be conducted at least twice annually on fire safety plans and evacuation procedures.

b.   All personnel shall be required to attend at least one class annually.

c.   Records shall contain, but not be limited to the dates of the classes, instructors, subject(s) reviewed, times begun and adjourned, personnel attending, and any other information deemed necessary and appropriate.

d.   All such records shall be in writing, signed, and dated, by the person conducting the class, and submitted to the administration within seventy-two (72) hours of the completion of such training class.

17.   Fire Classes

a.   Fire classes shall be conducted for all personnel on an annual basis. These shall not be in lieu of scheduled fire drills.

b.   Fire classes shall include, as a minimum, the following: the use of fire extinguishers; fire prevention; evacuation procedures; methods of removal; sounding the alarm; and other topics as appropriate.

c.   Records shall be maintained that reflect the attendance, course of study, and so on of all fire classes conducted.

d.   Such records shall be filed with the administration within seventy-two (72) hours of the completion of the training class.

e.   Fire classes shall be recorded on the Record of Training Class form.

f.   The person conducting the class shall be responsible for completing the Record of Training Class form and forwarding it to the appropriate departments.

Figure 7–3
(*Continued*)

18. Fire Alarm System

   a. Manual Pull Station

   This facility is equipped with manual fire alarm pull stations that will automatically sound the fire alarm system when activated. They are strategically located throughout the facility and all personnel shall be trained in their use at regularly scheduled training classes and drills. Our fire alarm system is connected to a fire alarm monitoring company that automatically notifies the fire station when an alarm is activated.

   b. Heat and Smoke Detectors

   Heat and smoke detectors are located throughout the building and will sound an alarm when activated; they will automatically notify our fire alarm monitoring company and thus the fire station when activated.

   c. Fire Zones

   A fire zone panel is located at the main entrance of the library. When a fire occurs that automatically activates the fire alarm system, an indicator light on the fire zone panel will show the area in which the fire is located. When a fire alarm is sounded, it is important that the fire zone panel be immediately checked to determine the areas where the fire is located.

19. Fire Alarm Signals

   a. Audible Alarm Signals

   This facility is equipped with an automatic, audible fire alarm signal that when activated will sound a continuous, loud, ringing sound until the fire alarm system has been reset. This automatic system will sound an alarm at the fire monitoring company when activated within the facility. The fire alarm zone panel in the main entrance of the library will indicate the zone in which the fire is located so that prompt action can be taken.

   b. Visual Alarm Signal

   A visual alarm signal for the hearing impaired has been provided so they will know when this facility is conducting a fire drill or when an actual emergency arises. These devices are located above each fire alarm bell and will activate simultaneously with the audible alarm signal. A blinking red light will indicate that a drill or actual emergency is in progress. All procedures must be followed as outlined within this section.

Figure 7–3
(*Continued*)

c. Code Alarm Signal
Should the fire alarm system fail to activate the automatic alarm signal, this facility shall use a voice alarm signal. The voice alarm system adopted by this facility shall be: "There is a fire emergency." This will include the location of that emergency. The person assigned communications procedures, as outlined within this manual, shall be responsible for notifying the Fire Department.

20. Fire Prevention

a. Fire prevention is the responsibility of all personnel and visitors alike.

b. Should anyone discover a fire hazard, or conditions that may create a fire hazard, prompt notification to the Director or designee shall be made of such conditions.

c. The Library Director or the designee shall be responsible for prompt investigation of such conditions and corrections to be made. All such hazardous conditions shall be corrected immediately.

d. Any hazardous condition requiring more than twenty-four (24) hours to correct shall be reported to the Director, in writing, by the responsible department supervisor, outlining what corrections will be made, the methods of correction, and when the hazardous conditions will be corrected.

21. Emergency Telephone Numbers

a. Facility Personnel
This library has developed a list of personnel, their addresses, phone numbers, and sections, for use during emergency or disaster situations. In addition, this list includes the names and home and business numbers of the next-of-kin who should be called in case of a personnel emergency. Information recorded on this list shall be classified as confidential and shall not be used for any other purpose. A copy of this information is located at each supervisor's station and in the administrative offices.

b. Medical Personnel
A listing of emergency medical personnel, such as paramedics, hospitals, physicians, and nurses, has been developed for use during emergency situations. This listing has the name of the individual, the institution with which she is associated, and the telephone number. A copy is located in each supervisor's office and in the administrative offices.

Figure 7–3
(*Continued*)

c. Auxiliary Support Personnel

In addition to the above, there are listings for Civil Defense, Police Department, state offices, rescue squads, utility companies, ambulances, and so on that may be necessary for an emergency or disaster situation. The listing contains the name of contact personnel and their telephone numbers. This listing is also kept in each supervisor's office and in the administrative offices.

d. Miscellaneous Information

All emergency call information shall be verified at least quarterly and corrections shall be made as necessary. These changes shall be filed within each department within twenty-four (24) hours of their correction. The Library Director shall designate the person who will be responsible for ensuring emergency call information is kept as current as possible.

22. Floor Plans

a. A floor plan of the library is posted throughout the building for all persons to review from time to time and shall not be removed unless authorized by the Director.

b. All staff members and volunteer workers shall be oriented to the design and the location of the floor plans.

c. Floor plans indicate all exits, evacuation routes, assembly areas, fire alarm pull stations, fire extinguishers, and other pertinent data necessary to the safety and well-being of all persons within the facility.

23. Fire and Smoke Barrier Doors

a. This facility is equipped with automatic fire and safety barrier doors so that a safer environment may be provided during an actual emergency.

b. Fire and smoke barrier doors must be closed at all times.

c. Fire and smoke barrier doors shall not be blocked at any time.

d. Should anyone discover a fire or smoke barrier door that is partially open or does not close properly, such as dragging or not fitting properly when the door is closed, she shall immediately report such findings to the Director.

e. Fire and smoke barrier doors will display a sign that reads "Fire Exit—Keep Door Closed" and it shall be visible only in the direction of exit travel.

Figure 7–3
(Continued)

---

24. Smoking Regulations

    a.   Smoking shall not be permitted within this facility, or anytime during a drill or actual emergency, even if evacuation has occurred and personnel are outside the building.

    b.   All hazardous areas shall be clearly identified with "No Smoking" signs.

    c.   All personnel will be made aware of these regulations during orientation, and the information will be repeated during fire classes. Violators of the regulation are subject to disciplinary action as outlined within the library's personnel policy manual.

    d.   "No Smoking" signs will be prominently displayed throughout the library.

25. All Clear Announcement

    a.   The All Clear signal adopted by our facility shall be a verbal announcement of "Code Green" or "All Clear."

    b.   The All Clear signal shall be used only when it has been determined, by the person in charge and by the Fire Department's Officer in Charge, that danger no longer exists.

    c.   Until the All Clear is given, patrons are not to be allowed to return into the library.

    d.   The fire area must be inspected by the Fire Department to ensure that the fire is out, that smoke and toxic gasses have been removed, and that the area is safe for the return of patrons and staff.

    e.   Only the person in charge shall be authorized to give the All Clear signal.

26. Communications Procedures

    a.   This facility shall implement emergency communications procedures should a fire or other disaster occur within the building or on the premises that could affect the safety and well-being of all concerned.

    b.   The person in charge, or his designee, shall be the only person authorized to release communications to the press and such releases shall be used only to expedite emergency procedures.

    c.   In order to expedite communications procedures, news bulletins may be issued to local television and radio stations indicating that a disaster has occurred and that emergency procedures are in place.

Figure 7–3
(*Continued*)

27. Damage to the Facility

Should the facility be damaged through fire or other disaster the Disaster Plan will be instituted immediately.

28. Safety Rules and Regulations

   a. Safety rules and regulations apply to emergency or disaster situations and such rules must be followed to prevent further injuries or reduce the possibility of injuries.

   b. All personnel are expected to carry out all procedures safely as instructed.

29. Call In Off-Duty Personnel

If a disaster or emergency occurs, the Library Director or the person in charge will determine whether additional staff are needed to manage the crisis or if off-duty staff should be notified not to report to work because of the situation. The library's personnel policy will dictate staff remuneration for this time.

30. Special Job Assignments

   a. During fire or other emergencies, special job assignments become necessary. Departments or individuals may be given specific responsibilities and shall be expected to carry out such assignments to the best of their ability.

   b. Special job assignments will be preassigned so staff members will know what is expected of them during a crisis.

31. Notification of Area Hospitals

   a. Should a fire or other disaster occur, the hospital shall be contacted and informed of the fire or other disaster and that injuries may result and be transported to the hospital.

   b. Should no injuries result from the fire or the disaster, the person in charge will notify the hospital that the alert be cancelled.

   c. Should a fire or other disaster occur that results in injuries, the person in charge, or her designee, shall notify the hospital of such injuries, the number of injuries, if known, and that the injured will be transported to their facility.

32. Searches and Search Teams

Should the situation arise for the need to conduct searches for injured or missing

Figure 7–3
(Continued)

patrons or personnel in the library, search teams shall be formed with the assistance and recommendations of local authorities.

33. Evacuation
Should it become necessary to evacuate the building, or any part thereof, evacuation routes and procedures shall be followed as established.

34. Exits

   a. The building is equipped with two or more exits. They are remote from each other and are designated on the floor plans posted throughout the facility.

   b. Primary and secondary exit routes have been preassigned for rapid and orderly evacuation purposes.

   c. It shall be the responsibility of all personnel to keep all exits clear at all times. Exit doors should never be blocked, even for a few moments.

   d. Any person discovering that an exit door has been blocked will clear the exit and report such violation to his immediate supervisor or the Library Director.

   e. Remember, exits are a means of escape. They can mean the difference between life or death. Keep exits clear and unobstructed at all times.

35. Assembly Areas

   a. Assembly areas have been preassigned for all personnel to use when evacuation is ordered.

   b. Assembly areas are designated on the floor plans posted throughout the building.

   c. Each exit has an assembly area related to it. Assembly areas must be used as assigned, unless otherwise instructed or emergency action requires other procedures to be taken.

36. Incident Reports

   a. When there is any incident that is accidental or related to any emergency or disaster, a written report must be filled out within twenty-four (24) hours.

   b. The Incident Report must be filled out by the person who witnessed the incident, accurately recording all information. The supervisor at the time of the incident should cosign the report.

Figure 7–3
(Continued)

   c.   The report shall be forwarded to all appropriate city or state offices within forty-eight (48) hours of the event.

   d.   A copy of the report shall be kept on file in the administration offices.

37. Hazardous Areas

   a.   Hazardous areas, such as power rooms, boiler rooms, and flammable liquid storage areas, will be identified as such.

   b.   "No Smoking" signs will be posted in all hazardous areas.

   c.   All hazardous areas are so designated on the floor plans posted throughout the facility.

38. Disaster Plans and Procedures
Should a fire or any other disaster occur within the library, the Disaster Plans and Procedures will be implemented immediately.

39. Fire Retardant Material Verification

   a.   All drapes, carpets, furniture and so on used in this library are flame resistant.

   b.   Manufacturers' Flame Test Ratings are on file in the administration offices and may be reviewed by interested personnel during normal business hours.

   c.   Periodic inspections shall be conducted by this facility for worn furnishings, torn or cut materials, and so forth. Such items shall be replaced or removed as quickly as possible.

40. Fire Safety Inspection

   a   The Library Director shall be responsible for conducting or having a designee conduct a Fire Safety Inspection on a quarterly basis.

   b.   A Fire Inspection Record shall be filed within forty-eight (48) hours after the inspection, listing all areas inspected and the results of such inspection.

   c.   Such entries shall be recorded in the administration offices.

   d.   The Fire Department shall annually conduct an unannounced fire safety inspection in accordance with current laws and file a written report of such inspection within forty-eight (48) hours.

Figure 7–3
(*Continued*)

41. Removal of Vehicles During Emergencies

    a. Should a fire or other disaster occur at the library, and the use of emergency vehicles becomes necessary, any vehicle blocking access to the building shall be removed prior to the arrival of emergency vehicles, so action can be taken without delay.

    b. Every effort will be made to locate the owner of the vehicle(s) so that vehicle(s) can be removed without damage. Should the owner not be located, or emergency action is necessary for immediate removal, this library shall have the power and authority to remove such vehicles by the most expedient means available.

    c. Every effort will be made to prevent damage to any vehicle(s) removed. A detailed inspection shall be made of any vehicle, noting any damage found. Such report shall be provided to the owner of the vehicle prior to the owner's removing the vehicle from the premises.

    d. When emergency or disaster situations exist at the library, local law enforcement agencies shall be responsible for providing traffic control procedures.

    e. In the event alternative transportation is needed, local law enforcement agencies, related health care facilities, national guard units, and so on will be contacted for their assistance.

    f. Request for alternative transportation must be coordinated through the staff assigned for such functions.

42. Emergency Control of Utilities

    a. All supervisors will be knowledgeable about the location and the use of the main power switches and emergency power systems.

    b. Flashlights for emergency use will be located in every department.

43. Fire Extinguishers

    a. Fire extinguishers are located throughout the facility. Their location is indicated on the floor plans.

    b. All staff shall familiarize themselves with the locations so action can be taken when needed.

    c. Fire extinguishers shall be inspected monthly and replaced, refilled, or rechanged when an inspection reveals such action is needed.

Figure 7–3
(Continued)

d. The local fire authority or other authorized agents shall conduct a yearly inspection of all fire extinguishers and the results of their findings shall be recorded and provided to the Library Director.

e. Fire extinguishers shall not be removed from their locations except when in actual use. If removal is necessary to replace or recharge a unit, another one must be put into its place before removal can occur.

f. Any person discovering that a fire extinguisher is missing from its location shall immediately report such information to her supervisor, who will inform the Library Director for replacement.

g. Fire extinguishers shall not be installed on walls, and so on to exceed five (5) feet from the floor to the top of the extinguisher.

h. Any fire extinguisher that has been used (that is, for demonstration or drill) shall not be restored to its location until it has been recharged.

i. A record of monthly fire extinguisher inspections shall be recorded and kept in the administration offices.

j. In-service training and fire training classes shall be conducted in the use of fire extinguishers.

44. Treatment of the Injured

a. Injuries sustained during an emergency may need treatment.

b. Only those injuries that are minor and can be treated properly by trained staff will be treated at the library. All others will be transferred to a local hospital.

45. Emergency Generator Test (if your facility has one)

a. Should the normal supply of power at the library be disrupted, this facility is equipped with an emergency generator system that will automatically activate within ten (10) seconds of the loss of the normal power supply.

b. Systems connected to the emergency generator are: emergency lighting; fire alarm and emergency alarms; exit signs; hall lights; septic pumps.

c. The emergency generator shall be tested on a weekly basis and such test results shall be recorded in the administration offices.

46. Fire Alarm Pull Stations

a. This library is equipped with an automatic fire alarm system that will acti-

Figure 7–3
(Continued)

vate when a loss of power occurs, when pull stations are activated, or when fire, smoke, or excessive heat are detected within the building.

b. Fire alarm pull stations are located throughout the building and locations are indicated on the floor plan.

c. The pull stations are red in color and have instructions for their use on the device.

d. Should you discover a fire, proceed to the nearest pull station, after you have evacuated any patrons from the immediate danger area, and activate the alarm as instructed.

e. Fire alarm zone panels are located at the front of the library near the circulation desk. When the alarm is activated, the zone in which the fire alarm was sounded will light up on the panel.

f. Once the alarm has sounded, assume your duties as assigned or that may be issued by the person in command.

g. The alarm will continue to sound until the fire alarm pull station activated has been reset or the alarm system has been disconnected.

h. At least one fire alarm pull station shall be tested monthly and a record of such shall be recorded in the administration offices.

47. Testing of the Fire Alarm System

a. A monthly test shall be conducted of the fire alarm system to ensure that it remains operable at all times.

b. The Library Director or the Facilities Manager shall conduct the test and be responsible for notifying the Fire Department when a test is being conducted and when it has been completed.

c. Testing devices and locations shall vary from month to month to ensure that all systems are operable.

d. A written record shall be maintained of the test results and kept on file in the administration offices.

48. Conducting a Fire Alarm System Test

a. The following procedure shall be used in conducting the monthly alarm test:

Figure 7–3
(Continued)

Notify the Fire Department and Alarm Company that a test is being conducted.

Select the device for testing.

Select the location for testing (must not be the same device or location used in the last testing period).

Station one person at the fire alarm unit to reset the system after testing is concluded.

Activate the alarm.

Record information as indicated on the test record.

Reset alarm system.

Contact the Fire Department and Alarm Company. Inform them that the test has been completed. Ask if the alarm sounded at the fire station. Record this information on the test record.

Complete the test record, and file the report in the administration offices.

b.   On a semiannual basis, the Library Director, with the assistance of the Fire Department's Fire Prevention Bureau, shall conduct a test of all emergency equipment maintained and installed within the facility.

49. Storage Areas

a.   All storage areas shall be kept free from accumulation of trash, rubbish, rags, paper, and so on at all times.

b.   Paint, flammable liquids, and so on shall not be stored in areas where intense heat or open flame devices could ignite such matter. Metal storage cabinets are recommended for this purpose.

c.   Cleaning supplies and so on shall be stored in separate areas, preferably in a metal storage cabinet. All products shall be labeled accordingly.

50. Inspection of Heat and Air-Condition Systems

a.   Prior to each heating and cooling season, all systems shall be inspected for possible leaks, broken lines, and so forth.

b.   The Library Director shall be responsible for such inspection and shall have the authority to hire approved vendors to assist in making the inspection when such assistance is necessary.

Figure 7–3
(Continued)

51. Electrical Appliances

   a. All electrical appliances (toasters, microwaves, and so on) permitted to be in the library are in good working order and UL approved.

   b. Staff is required to report any items that have frayed cords or other imperfections for replacement.

   c. The use of extension cords is discouraged.

52. Review of Fire Plans and Evacuation Procedures:

   a. Fire, disaster, and evacuation procedures outlined in this manual, and as established by this library, shall be reviewed at least annually.

   b. Such plans and procedures shall be reviewed by the Safety Risk Committee, as well as law enforcement agencies and the Fire Department for their comments on the content and effectiveness of the plan.

   c. The Library Director shall maintain a file on such reviews and the changes that were implemented as a result of the reviews.

Figure 7–4
Disaster Response Team

We recommend that every library have a disaster response team that can plan strategies in advance of an emergency and is thus prepared if one should occur. A "telephone tree" is usually an effective way to reach people, either inside the library building itself or when there are no staff members present. People share in the notification of team members in an orderly fashion so that everyone who needs to be alerted is. The number of members on the list may vary from library to library, but it should usually include the following:

Director

Department supervisors

Security personnel

Maintenance personnel

Others who may be included:

City manager or mayor, or appropriate official

Board president

Police chief

Fire chief

Figure 7–5				
Fire Inspection Record				
Fire Inspection Record **Inspected by:**_____ **Date:**_____				
Area inspected	**Problem notes**	**Corrective action needed**	**Whose responsibility**	**Correction completion date**

Figure 7–6
Fire Drill Report

Date:_____Day of the week:_____Location/Place:_____

Time drill (evacuation) was initiated: a.m._____ p.m. _____

The drill was a: planned drill:_____   unplanned drill (false alarm):_____

If unplanned, was the director notified? Yes_____ No _____

          At what time_____

Location of simulated fire origin: _____

Escape paths used in the drill: _____

Estimated number of people involved in the drill: _____

Rate evaluation time: _____ Prompt (3 min. or less)

                          _____ Slow (Over 3 min., but not in excess of 13 min.)

                          _____ Impractical (more than 13 min.)

1.   Reason for fire drill:

2.   Was evacuation conducted in a safe and efficient manner? If not, explain.

3.   Detail any potential or actual difficulties to safe and efficient evacuation. How
     might the evacuation time be improved?

4.   Do staff give evidence of knowledge of evacuation procedure? If not, detail.

5.   Comments relating to patrons or staff who resisted or failed to participate in
     the fire drill:

6.   Recommended follow-up:

                         Staff member _____

                         Signature   Date

Figure 7–7
Fire Alarm Work Report

Date:_____Day of the week:_____Location/Place:_____

Time of initial call for service: _____

Requested by: _____

Time of service: _____

Time fire department notified: _____

Reason for service:

Description of work completed:

Follow-up needed:

Fire department input:

Closure date:

                                      Staff member _____

                                        Signature   Date

                                        Reviewed by the director

                                        _____

                                        Signature   Date

Figure 7–8
Monthly Emergency Equipment Inspection Report

Emergency Equipment   Inspected by:_____

Emergency equipment	Month	Available	Problems/ Repairs needed	Action taken
Flashlights with batteries				
Extra set of batteries				
Rope				
Cutting implements				
Medical/first aid kit				
Water				
Candles				
Emergency light system				
2–way radio or cell phone				

Figure 7–9				
Monthly Fire Extinguisher Inspection Record				
Inspected by:_____Date:_____				
Location	**At full pressure?**	**Refilled?**	**Replaced?**	**Properly tagged?**

8 Arranging Space and Considerations for Special Needs Patrons

8.1 Making the Most of Space

Every library should review the changing needs of its community and how they will affect the facility itself at least every five years. This chapter is designed to assist you in calculating those requirements, based on the needs of equipment placement, work areas, materials storage and handling areas, and support space. Each of these is determined in a slightly different manner. With the change in the way information is being stored, space requirements are different now, but we do not necessarily need to have additions to our libraries. With money being tight, it is often not feasible for us to do so or build new libraries. Rather, we have subscribed to the idea that renovation and retrofitting are the way to proceed. Reassigning space for other functions is more and more the norm, and the facilities manager is one of the key planners in assisting the library director in adapting current space for other purposes.

There are three major categories into which our space requirements fall. These are equipment space, support and program space, and administrative space.

Equipment space—be it bookshelves or workstations—must be given the first consideration in looking at space requirements. All the other space within a facility is related to this primary use. The basic unit for equipment space is a module—what is required for one unit, one desk, and so on. You need to know the sum of the space required by all of the modules in order to arrive at the final calculation for equipment space.

Support space is the work area that surrounds the needed modules. This might include a storage room or even a staff lounge. Space for all the mechanical needs is also included in this category.

Administrative space is the space that is required for supervision, quality control, customer service, personnel, and other management functions, as well as the space needed for the collection and user seating. Program and meeting space is another area that the facilities manager or the library director will need to consider. This is the space that is required to hold or host public meetings, small or large gatherings, or public performances. In addition to having the appropriate furniture to accommodate these various uses, one of the most crucial issues regarding this type of space is the need to have alternative means of egress from the rooms in case of a fire or other disaster.

It is with these functions in mind that the facilities manager should work with management to consider how currently available space might be readily adapted to provide more room without the large investment of construction. The first question the facilities manager should raise is whether optimum use is already being made. While the floor may be crowded, there may, in fact, be a lot of unused space on the walls. Can shelves or storage racks be added to increase wall use? Can a mezzanine be built over office or work areas? Would different equipment open up more space?

The next aspect to address is work schedules. Is it possible that flex schedules could help accommodate the need for additional workstations? Can they be shared or is it imperative that each person have a separate workstation? Would these changes impact productivity? Is the space arrangement influencing work flow?

Another consideration that must be reviewed is the changing formats of materials. With the increased use of digital technology, libraries may not need as much space to retain particular formats or types of information. Can this space then be redesigned to accommodate another function?

Improving your facility's space use begins with an objective analysis of current use in your library. This will give you an accurate picture of how you are using the building at present and what additional capacity may be required to smooth out the flow of work or anticipate increased workloads.

8.2   Adaptive Reuse

Because many of our library buildings were designed before current standards for access were implemented and before there were so many computers and other technology in the workplace, renovations may be needed to make facilities appropriate for current use. The library director has to evaluate the current service needs and find ways to adapt usable space so that it is efficient and effective for new uses. This process is generally referred to as retrofitting or adaptive reuse. In addition, there are other elements that must be taken into consideration that are directly related to the age of the building. These include the former old standards, asbestos, sanitation, and lead paint.

In the time that has elapsed from original construction to the present, there will have been changes in code regulations. The local fire marshal and building inspectors will be good sources of information on state and local requirements that must be met.

The facilities manager definitely will need to have input into the process of retrofitting, and may, in fact, even be assigned responsibilities in relation to it. However, this is beyond the scope of this volume. Texts that deal with construction specifics must be consulted.

8.3   The Role of the Facilities Manager in Determining Space Needs

The facilities manager has an important role to play not only in determining solutions to space needs through adaptation of the current building, but also in providing input for new construction. Changing the use of current space may have an impact in the ongoing facilities management program. This may be due to additional cleaning, electrical, or other technical updating that is needed. With more space, there will be additional upkeep, and from a planning perspective, it would be wise to involve the individuals who will be expected to perform these duties. There may be materials that are easier to clean than others and arrangements that will be easier to maintain that should be considered in the planning stages. Having input at the outset is a much more efficient way of managing future maintenance issues than waiting until after the adaptation or the addition of space is completed.

The facilities manager has an important job in the reorganizing of space to suit the needs of the services the library is planning to provide. While it is critical that the facilities manager is involved from the outset, it is not our intention here to outline the planning process. There are other suitable documents, including the Public Library Association's manuals, that more than fill this role. As a partner of the library director, the facilities manager can be of immense assistance in helping the staff understand what the current structure will allow and what adaptations may be possible based on the basic physical structure. For more than simple renovations, a building committee is advisable so individuals can contribute their expertise in particular areas.

The design of the physical facility and the arrangement of the materials, meeting space, and other rooms are critical to the achievement of the library's goals. The facilities manager should have the ability to look at space and visualize the service functions that might take place in a given area. Properly designed lighting, as well as the placement of furniture and displays, can help the library create an environment that is welcoming to users.

Discussion and redefinition of the library's role will indicate the direction the library will take. The director and the facilities manager should know the answers to questions such as, "Will the library be used as a cultural center for the arts, for crafts, for exhibitions?" Or, "Will the library be a center of independent learning and continuing education in the community?" What special features of the facility will be needed to address these functions? The facilities manager should be able to look at the identified needs with the director and collect the facts on the various types of building improvements that might be possible and their costs.

Physical facilities problems can be addressed by observing the present use of the building. A photographic or video record is helpful in highlighting overcrowded conditions, poor lighting, areas of uncomfortable air circulation, temperature and humidity problems, shabby or uncomfortable furniture, barriers to the disabled, depressing colors, peeling paint, inconvenient and unsafe entrances, and so on. The facilities manager can be useful to the director in collecting this type of data, researching alternatives, and making suggestions for improvements.

8.4   Space Planning Steps

Improving a library to satisfy present or projected space needs begins with an objective analysis of major operations. This analysis must provide a picture of present capacity, a projection of anticipated capacity, and a recommendation on how to proceed with satisfying the needs. Why bother with all this time-consuming information gathering? The result will truly be worth the effort.

Documenting present conditions in the facility is the place to start. Planning for effective library facilities first of all takes into consideration the current population of the area and projects future growth. Usually, you will be able to obtain this information from the appropriate municipal office and from the local school district.

Projecting the space needed to accommodate the collection has gotten a little trickier over the past few years with the introduction of new storage media. The number of books that can be stored per square foot varies depending upon the height of the shelving and the width of the aisles. Traditionally, it was recommended that the size of the collection be measured using a per capita estimate and then calculating projected space by adding the average number of net purchases over a period of time (usually 20–25 years). Add in the variations for audiovisuals and compact disc storage and the formula changes! However, the facilities manager and the library director must take into consideration the type of equipment that will be used to keep the new media organized as well.

Adequate seating is determined by type. During construction or renovation the following information may be helpful. If study carrels will be used, an area of 30 square feet is needed. If lounge chairs will be provided, the estimate is then at 35 square feet. Seating in meeting rooms is somewhat different, depending upon the arrangement of chairs, tables, and other furniture. For a lecture setting, the rule of thumb is to multiply 10 square feet by the number of seats desired. For seating at a conference table, you will need 25 square feet times the number of seats desired. To determine the overall number of seats to be made available estimate 5 for every 1,000 people in the population area. If you are in a library now and are not sure of the numbers that can be accommodated in your space, a phone call to the local fire department is warranted. We have found them to be of great assistance in helping establish a safe, comfortable seating plan for these areas.

Workstations include the service points where staff interact with the public and quiet places to work away from the flow of patron traffic. The library director will need to evaluate present staff workloads and trends in current service patterns in order to make a decision on the appropriate amount of space that should be set aside for workstations. Prospective departments or service areas will also need to be considered. This process makes us focus on the *tasks* that are to be performed in a given area of the library and on the way these tasks relate to other library operations. We will then be able to project the amount of space to allocate, estimating that approximately 150 square feet per workstation will be needed to create a comfortable work area.

Meeting room and special use space must also be examined. Library planners should also understand that the need for space is not the only reason for examining physical facilities. Energy efficiency and the condition of the heating, ventilating, and air-conditioning systems; handicapped accessibility; adaptability to meet the electrical and telecommunications requirements; and the general effectiveness of work flow are all suitable reasons to examine the facility.

The following is a selected list of representative furnishings and the respective space allocations that are appropriate for their use. All are given in square feet. This information was taken from the *Library Space Planning Guide*, which is a free publication of the Connecticut State Library. We also recommend the use of *The Americans with Disabilities Act Handbook*, edited by Maureen Harrison and Steve Gilbert, and *Building Blocks for Libraries Spaces: Functional Guidelines*, published by the American Library Association.

Space and Furnishing	**Sq. ft.**
Small-group study room	25 per seat
Modular AV storage unit	15 per unit
Atlas/dictionary stand	30
Microfilm reader/printer	30
Microfilm cabinet	10 per unit
Index table	140
Vertical file	10 per unit
Staff lounge	50, with additional 25 per seat
Paperback rack	35
Newspaper rack	25
Public access catalog terminal	30
Display case	50
Public access microcomputer	60
Photocopier	50
Three-foot single-face bookstack display	10
Compact disc/cassette/video display	30
Three-foot locking cabinet	15

New facilities, additions, or major modifications require large investments of both time and money. When there is a perceived need for new or expanded space in a library, it is important that the library director and the facilities manager perform this careful study to determine if the needs actually reflect the perceptions. These steps will save time and money in the long run because there may be some options in reassigning space; there may be some relatively inexpensive ways of putting unused space into operation (for example, adding a mez-zanine rather than a full addition); or, it may be determined that the most cost-effective path to take is building a new structure!

Figure 8–1
Checklist for Space Planning

- service area population

- collection space

- user seating space

- staff work stations

- meeting room needs

- special use space

- nonassignable (mechanical room) space

- parking needs

8.5   Addressing Special Needs

Most library buildings predate the passage of the Americans with Disabilities Act of June 1990, which went into effect in 1992. Title II (regarding public entities) prohibits discrimination not only of those who may want to use our facilities, but also of those who are qualified and want to work in our libraries. This legislation directed that administrators of public buildings make reasonable accommodations to address the needs of individuals who are physically challenged.

Clearly, a main goal of a public library is to ensure that we make our services accessible to everyone. Accessibility can be best defined as providing a barrier-free environment for all who want to use our services. Furthermore, there is a growing senior population that may have some difficulties opening doors, and so on, due to common ailments like arthritis. Making some changes in the facility will encourage this population to increase its use. Detailed information about the legislation is available in the Public Law, 101–336 (U.S. Senate sec. 933 May 5, 1989).

While all public buildings were supposed to be in compliance by 1995, we recognize that there are some libraries, among many other buildings, that have still not been able to make the necessary changes. However, the reason for this is not a lack of sensitivity or concern for those with disabilities, but rather a lack of the resources or local conditions needed to make the improvements. This has often stalled the process, but improvements may not necessarily be expensive.

It is imperative that libraries pay attention to the guidelines that have been set up and prioritize improvements that must be made to the facility in order to accommodate special needs. In general, the highest priority should be given to making sure people are able to enter the building. The next priority is enabling patrons to get to those areas where services are available. They should be able to move freely within the structure and be able to use the rest rooms.

8.6 Low-Cost Solutions for Reasonable Accommodations at the Job Site

The Americans with Disabilities Act applies to staff and potential staff as well as to all of our patrons. It is therefore prudent for the facilities management staff to consider components of the building that may be hindrances, or perhaps even potentially dangerous, to someone with a disability. It is advisable to consult someone who has experience in the special needs area. There may be someone in your town's personnel, legal, or human rights department who will be able to assist you with specifics in this area.

Physical Accommodations

Physical accommodations can often be made to the immediate job site to enable people to carry out essential job functions. These may include alterations to the actual work environment or simply the provision of certain equipment. Some accommodations may be classified as high tech. These include sophisticated robotic devices, speech synthesizers, environmental control systems, and computerized reading machines.

Low-tech accommodations include raising a worker's desk so a wheelchair will fit under it, providing a telephone amplifier for someone with a hearing impairment, or installing a page-turning device for someone who might have limited use of his hands.

The Job Accommodation Network is a nationwide toll-free information service for employers, and almost 70 percent of the accommodations they suggest cost $500 or less.

Other Types of Accommodations

Accommodations may be nonphysical in nature. An example of this is adjusting the work schedule and assignments for a worker who may need to rest between work periods or may require periodic medical treatment. There should be training for supervisors and coworkers to help them understand an employee's disability. As with physical accommodations, changes such as these allow workers with disabilities to carry out the essentials of their job. This is the essence of the ADA legislation—providing the environment and opportunity for a qualified worker to do her job.

Figure 8–2
Checklist for Compliance with the ADA Code

Parking

Are spaces clearly identified?

Is there a 12-foot minimum width?

Is the surface level?

Are there curb cuts for easy movement?

Are the spaces as close as possible to the accessible entry?

Is a sign posted indicating there is handicapped parking?

Walkways

Are the surfaces at least 48 inches wide?

Is the gradient 5 percent?

Is there a continuous common surface with no abrupt changes or steps?

Is the level platform 5 feet by 5 feet if the door swings out, 3 feet by 5 feet if the door doesn't swing out?

Do the walkways extend more than 1 foot beside each side of the door?

Ramps

Is the slope no greater than 1 foot for every 12 feet?

Is there a handrail on one side?

Is the handrail 32 inches from the surface?

Is the surface smooth and nonslip?

Are there level platforms at 30-foot intervals for rest and safety?

Entrances and Exits

Is there at least one that can accommodate the width of a wheelchair?

Is it near an elevator if one is necessary to use the building?

Is there signage to identify the accessible entrance?

Doors

Are they no less than 32 inches when open?

Is there a 5–foot minimum level area on a pull side, 4–foot on a push side?

Are they operable by a single effort, with reasonable pressure?

Figure 8–2
(Continued)

Is the floor level? Does it extend 1 foot beyond each side of the door?

Is the threshold $^1/_4$ inch or less but not more than $^1/_2$ inch. More than $^1/_2$ inch may require a ramp.

Are abrupt changes avoided?

Are there enough appropriate means of egress from all rooms in case of emergency?

What is the pound-force needed to open a door? Optimum is 5 pounds.

Are door knobs lever-type rather than rounded?

Stairs

Are handrails 32 inches from the tread?

Are steps 7 inches or less?

Does one handrail extend 18 inches beyond the top and bottom step?

Rest Rooms

Are there a significant number?

Is there a turning space of 60 inches by 60 inches?

Is the stall 3 feet wide by 4 feet 8 inches deep? Is there a space of 48 inches between the wall and the front of the stall?

Is the door 32 inches wide, and does it swing out?

Are there 1 $^1/_2$–inch grab bars on each side? Is there a 1$^1/_2$–inch clearance between the rail and the wall? Is it fastened securely at the ends and at the center?

Is the commode 33 inches from the floor? Is toilet paper accessible in front or beside the user?

Are drain pipes and hot water pipes covered or insulated?

Are mirrors and shelves no higher than 40 inches?

Are towel racks, dispensers, disposal units no higher than 40 inches from the floor, and at the side of the lavatory, not above it?

Watercoolers

Are these placed 36 inches or less from the floor?

Can they be used by someone in a wheelchair?

Figure 8–2
(Continued)

Public Phones

Can someone reach to dial? Are they placed 48 inches or less from the floor?

Is the coin slot reachable?

No protrusions from the wall should be 4 feet or longer.

Elevator

Are the controls 48 inches or less from the floor?

Are the buttons labeled with raised letters?

Are the controls easy to push?

Is the cab at least 5 feet by 5 feet?

Controls

Are the switches and controls for light, heat, ventilation, windows, fire alarms, and all similar controls within the reach of individuals in a wheelchair? (no more than 48 inches from the floor)

Identification

Are numbers and letters in either raised or recessed form?

Are all identification signs between 4 feet 6 inches to 5 feet high measured from the floor to the right or left of any door?

Warning Signals

Are there audible and simultaneous visual signals for hearing- or sight-impaired?

Are exit signs identifiable?

Hazard Areas

Are visual and tactile alerts in place?

Service Desks

Are service desks at a height that will have staff at eye level with patrons who are in wheelchairs so that the staff will not be looking down on them? There must be a 3–foot section at each desk that is at handicapped-accessible height.

Figure 8–2
(Continued)

Seating and Workstations

Are these at a height that is appropriate for use by someone in a wheelchair? There must be 5 percent of every type of seating that is accessible.

Equipment

Does the library have any specialized equipment that can be used by people with special needs? (Example: voice-activated computer)

8.7   Other Barriers to Library Access

Another barrier that may be present in the library that, while not directly connected to the structure of the building, leaves a lasting impression on patrons, is the attitude of the staff. It is the responsibility of the library director to set the tone for the inclusion of all patrons in the library. A training session should be held for the staff so they can be sensitized to the needs of patrons who have various challenges. Staff should also be taught simple, yet empathetic strategies so they are able to make people feel welcome and comfortable in the library. Equipment that may be considered includes but is not limited to a wheelchair, adaptive software to assist patrons with sight impairments or learning disabilities, and amplifiers for patrons with difficulty in hearing. A good strategy to use in the training session is role playing. Have some staff wear a blindfold, sit in a wheelchair, or use earplugs. Then have other staff members interact with the "disabled" member and then get their feedback. The firsthand results are surprising and a very powerful tool to use with staff to have them understand the needs of patrons with disabilities.

Customers with disabilities should be able to arrive at the site, approach the building, and enter the library as freely as everyone else. The following pages include schematic drawings that can be used by the library to ensure that the facility meets the approved code. They should be helpful in clarifying these needs. For more information on this subject, see the document released by the Department of Justice, "Nondiscrimination on the Basis of Disability by Public Accommodations and Commercial Facilities, Final Rule" in the *Federal Register* 54, no. 144 (July 26, 1991): 356–376.

Figure 8–3
ADA Guidelines: Getting Into the Facility

Parking (ADAAG 4.6)

POTENTIAL SOLUTIONS

1. **Are an adequate number of accessible parking spaces available (8 feet wide for car plus 5-foot striped access aisle)?** (ADAAG 4.6.1; 4.1.2(5))

✓ Reconfigure a reasonable number of spaces by repainting stripes.

NOTE: Outpatient medical care facilities must have a higher number of accessible spaces, totalling 10% of all spaces. (ADAAG 4.1.2.(5)(d))

NOTE: One in eight accessible spaces must be van accessible.

NOTE: *Older persons benefit from a protected pathway through the parking area to the facility. A pathway can be protected from vehicular traffic using pavement markings, planting, or drainage strips, etc.*

ADA Standards requirements for new construction and alterations:	
Total spaces	**Accessible spaces**
1 to 25	1 space
26 to 50	2 spaces
51 to 75	3 spaces
76 to 100	4 spaces

Up to 500 total spaces, add 1 space per 100 additional spaces.

2. **Are 8-foot-wide spaces with 98" of vertical clearance available for lift-equipped vans?** (ADAAG 4.1.2.5(b); 4.6.5)

✓ Reconfigure to provide at least one of the required number of van-accessible spaces. At least one of every eight accessible spaces must be van-accessible. If there is only one space, that must be van-accessible.

3. **Are the accessible spaces closest to the accessible entrance?** (ADAAG 4.6.2)

✓ Reconfigure spaces to minimize the length of walk to entrance.

4. **Are accessible spaces marked with the International Symbol of Accessibility? Are there signs reading "Van Accessible" at van spaces?** (ADAAG 4.6.4)

✓ Add signs, placed so that they are not obstructed by cars.

5. *Is there a policy on violations of accessible parking?*

✓ *Develop and enforce a policy to check for violators. Notify the proper authorities.*

Figure 8–4
ADA Guidelines: Path of Travel

1. **Does the exterior path of travel require the use of stairs?** (ADAAG 4.3.2)

   ✓ Add a ramp if the path of travel is interrupted by stairs.
   ✓ Add an alternative pathway on level or gently sloping ground.

2. **Are there curb cuts or ramps where there is a change in level greater than ½"?**
   (ADAAG 4.3.8)

   ✓ Install curb cuts at sidewalks, drop-offs, drives, or parking.
   ✓ Add small ramp up to the curb.

3. **Do exterior stairs in the path of travel have handrails on both sides?**

   ✓ Install handrails on both sides of the stairs in the path of travel.

4. **Is the path of travel and curb cut, stable, firm and slip-resistant?** (ADAAG 4.5; 4.3.8)

   ✓ Repair uneven paving. Fill small bumps and breaks with beveled patches.
   ✓ Replace gravel with hard top.
   ✓ Roughen existing surface.
   ✓ Replace curb cut material with nonslip paving, such as bituminous or broom-finish concrete.

5. **Is the path at least 36" wide?**
   (ADAAG 4.3.3)

   ✓ Modify landscaping or other features that narrow the path of travel.
   ✓ Widen the pathway.
   ✓ Relocate route of travel.

6. **Can all objects protruding into the path be detected by a person with a visual disability using a cane?** (ADAAG 4.4.1)

   ✓ Move or remove protruding objects.
   ✓ Add a cane-detectable base that extends to the ground or place a cane-detectable object underneath as a warning barrier.
   ✓ Trim overhanging branches that protrude into path of travel within 80" of the ground.

   NOTE: It is not necessary to remove objects that protrude less than 4" from the wall.

7. *If a pathway is long, are there benches or chairs for people to sit down if they have limited stamina?*

   ✓ *Place a bench or seating near a long pathway. Do not obstruct wheelchair access.*

8. **Are gratings located in the path?**
   (ADAAG 4.5.4)

   ✓ Replace gratings if they do not meet standard. (Spaces no wider than ½").
   ✓ Reposition the grating. The long sides of rectangular openings should be placed perpendicular to the direction of travel.

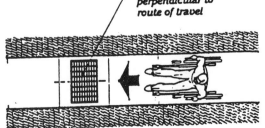

long dimension perpendicular to route of travel

16

Figure 8–5
ADA Guidelines: Entrances

POTENTIAL SOLUTIONS

1. **If there are stairs at the main entrance, is there also a ramp or lift?**
   ADAAG 4.1.3(8)(a); 4.14)

   NOTE: Do not use a service entrance as the accessible entrance unless there is no other option. Make sure there is accessible parking near accessible entrances.

   ✓ Add a ramp or lift.
   ✓ Create an alternative accessible entrance at or before inaccessible entrances.
   ✓ Install signs indicating the location of the nearest accessible entrance.
   (ADAAG 4.1.4(8)(d))

2. **Can the alternate accessible entrance be used independently?** (ADAAG 4.13)

   For example, eliminate as much as possible the need for assistance to answer a doorbell, to operate a lift, or to put down a temporary ramp.

   ✓ Modify entrance so that it can be used independently.
   ✓ If modification is not readily achievable, install call button to summon assistance.

3. **Does the entrance door have at least a 32" clear opening (for a double door, at least one leaf with 32" clear opening)?** (ADAAG 4.13.5)

   ✓ Widen the door.
   ✓ Install offset hinges which will add 1½" to door width.

4. **Are doormats 1/2" high or less, and secured to the floor at all edges?**
   (ADAAG 4.5.3)

   ✓ Replace or remove mats.
   ✓ Secure mats at edges.

5. **Can doors be opened with 5 foot pounds (5 lbf) or less of force?**
   (ADAAG 4.13.11)

   NOTE: You can use a fish scale to measure door's opening force by attaching one end to the door as it starts to open.

   ✓ Adjust the door closers.
   ✓ Oil the hinges.
   ✓ Install lighter doors.
   ✓ Install power-assisted or automatic door openers.
   ✓ Add bell to summon assistance.

Figure 8–6
ADA Guidelines: Ramps

POTENTIAL SOLUTIONS

1. **Are the slopes of ramps no steeper than 1:12?** (ADAAG 4.8.2)

   NOTE: 1:12 means for every 12 inches along the base of the ramp, the height increases 1." Many people prefer a more gradual slope if space is available. The least possible slope should be used for any ramp.

   ✓ Lengthen ramp to decrease slope.
   ✓ Relocate ramp.
   ✓ If space is limited, reconfigure ramp to include switchbacks.

2. **Do all ramps with drop-offs have curbs, walls, railings on both sides?** (ADAAG 4.8.7; 4.8.5)

   ✓ Add curbs, walls, railings, or projecting surfaces to the ramp to prevent persons from slipping off the ramp.

3. **Are railings sturdy and between 34" and 38" above ramp surface?** (ADAAG 4.9.4.(5))

   ✓ Adjust height of railings.
   ✓ Secure or replace railings.
   ✓ Dual handrails will allow wheelchair users to use the lower rails if the ramp is not too wide.

4. **Is width between railings at least 36 "?** (ADAAG 4.83)

   ✓ Relocate railings.
   ✓ Widen the ramp.

5. **Are ramp surfaces nonslip and even?** (ADAAG 4.5.1)

   ✓ Add nonskid adhesive strips.
   ✓ Resurface existing ramps using a broom finish or roughening the surface.

6. **Is there a 5-foot long level landing at every 30-foot horizontal length of ramp, at the top and bottom of ramps, and where the ramp changes direction?** (ADAAG 4.8.4)

   ✓ Relocate ramp.

7. **Does the ramp rise no more than 30 " between landings?** (ADAAG 4.8.2)

   ✓ Remodel ramp.

8. **Is the width of the gripping surface of the handrails 1¼ " to 1½ ", or does the shape provide an equivalent gripping surface?** (ADAAG 4.9.4; 4.26.2)

   ✓ Replace railings.

Figure 8–7
ADA Guidelines: Interior Doors

POTENTIAL SOLUTIONS

1. **Does the door have a 32" clear opening?** (ADAAG 4.13.5)

✓ Widen the door.
✓ Install offset hinges.

2. **Can doors be opened without too much force (5lbf maximum)?**

✓ Adjust door closers and oil the hinges.
✓ Install a lighter door.
✓ Install an automatic door opener.
✓ Add a bell to summon assistance.
✓ Adjust hinges to lighten the load.

3. **Is the door threshold less than 1/4 " or beveled?** (ADAAG 4.13.8; 4.5.2)

✓ Plane down the threshold.
✓ Add a bevel to the threshold.

4. **Are door handles 48" high (or less) and can they be opened with a closed fist?** (ADAAG 4.13.9)

✓ Lower door handle.
✓ Replace door handle with a lever or loop handle.
✓ Add a lever handle extension.
✓ Install power assisted or automatic door opener.

5. **Is there at least 18" of clear wall space on the pull side of the door, next to the handle?** (ADAAG 4.13.6)

✓ Reverse door swing so it can be pushed open.
✓ Add power-assisted door opener.
✓ Modify doorway.
✓ Move or remove obstructing partitions.

NOTE: A person using a walker or a wheelchair needs this space to get close enough to open the door.

Figure 8–8
ADA Guidelines: Lifts

POTENTIAL SOLUTIONS

1. **Is there a clear space of 30" by 48" front of lift?**
   (ADAAG 4.11.2; 4.2.4.1)

   ✓ Keep pathway clear to allow wheelchair use.

   ✓ Rearrange furniture or equipment to allow room to maneuver.

2. **Can the lift be operated easily and independently?** (ADAAG 4.11.3)

   ✓ Provide easy-to-read and complete instructions on operation and safety.

   ✓ Install call button to allow user to summon assistance. Assistant should be able to respond immediately.

3. **Can the lift be operated with one hand or with a closed fist?**
   (ADAAG 4.11.2; 4.27.4)

   ✓ Use levers or loop handle.

   ✓ Test for operation of 5 lbs or less.

4. **Are controls within reach for wheelchair user (15"- 48" high)?**
   (ADAAG 4.11.2;4.2.5;4.2.6)

   ✓ Move controls.

   ✓ Add extension levers to controls.

   ✓ If side approach to the lift, controls may be up to 54."

   ✓ If front approach, controls should be between 15" and 48."

5. **Is the lift platform at least 30" wide by 48" long?**
   (ADAAG 4.11.2; 4.2.4.1)

   ✓ Modify existing lift or replace with a lift platform capable of safely handling wheelchair.

Figure 8–9
ADA Guidelines: Signage

	POTENTIAL SOLUTIONS
1. **Do signs designating permanent rooms and spaces, such as restroom signs, exit signs, and room numbers, include Braille and raised lettering?** (ADAAG 4.30.4)	✓ Add signage that has raised and Braille letters, complies with finish and contrast standards, and is mounted at the correct height and location.
2. **Are signs mounted on the wall next to a door opening?** (ADAAG 4.30.6) NOTE: Tactile signage should never be installed on a door.	✓ Install on the wall adjacent to the latch side of the door.
3. **Are signs in high contrast print and visible from a distance?** (ADAAG 4.30.5)	✓ Make sure raised letters are also high in contrast to aid persons with low vision. ✓ Replace signs with small letters posted over doorways with more visible signs.
4. *Is the content of the signs clear to all persons?*	✓ *Replace or supplement unclear signs. For example, signs for public restrooms in a country theme restaurant which label the restrooms "hens" and "roosters."* ✓ *Add pictorial signage, using the international symbols where possible, to assist persons with cognitive disabilities.*

International
Accessibility Symbol

Braille
Symbol

Access for Individuals with
Blind or Low Vision

Figure 8–10
ADA Guidelines: Supplemental Services

Telephones (ADAAG 4.1.3(17);4.31)

1. **Is there clear floor space of at least 30" x 48" in front of at least one pay or public use phone?** (ADAAG 4.31.2)

   ✓ Move furnishings
   ✓ Replace booth with an open station.

2. **Is the highest operable part of the phone no higher than 48" (up to 54" if a side approach is possible)?** (ADAAG 4.31.3)

   ✓ Contact phone company to lower telephone.

3. *Is a chair available for someone who prefers to sit while making a call?*

   ✓ *Provide a lightweight, movable chair or stool.*

4. **Does the phone (pay phone or public) protrude no more than 4" into the circulation space?** (ADAAG 4.31.4;4.4.1)

   ✓ Place a cane-detectable barrier on each side.

5. **Does the phone have push-button controls, *and is the dialing panel well lit*?** (ADAAG 4.31.6)

   ✓ Contact phone company to convert dial panel and provide lighting at phone level.
   ✓ *Install overhead lighting.*
   ✓ *Provide horizontal shelf to place bags.*

6. **Is the phone hearing aid compatible and adapted for volume control?** (ADAAG 4.31.5)

   ✓ Contact the phone company to add an induction coil (T-switch) and volume control.

7. **Is there at least one public pay phone which is equipped with a text telephone (TTY or TTD)?** (ADAAG 4.31.9;4.1.3.(17);4.1.6(1)(e))

   ✓ Install a text telephone and/or provide a shelf and outlet for people to plug in their own TTYs.

8. **Are the phone and its features clearly identified?** (ADAAG 4.30.7(3);4.30.7(4))

   ✓ Add signage indicating volume control and/or TTY.

International
Volume Control Symbol:

International
TTY Symbol:

Assisted Listening
System:

Figure 8–11
ADA Guidelines: Drinking Fountains, Alarms, and Emergency Exits

---

1. **Is there at least one fountain with clear floor space of at least 30" x 48" front?** (ADAAG 4.15.5)

   ✓ Remove furnishings or provide another fountain in a more accessible area.

2. **Is there one fountain with its spout no higher than 36" from the ground, and another with a standard height spout (or a single "hi-lo" fountain)?** (ADAAG 4.15.2;4.1.3(10))

   ✓ Provide cup dispensers for fountains with spouts that are too high and/or an accessible water cooler.

3. **Are there controls mounted on the front or on a side near the front edge which are operable with one closed fist** *or the press of a foot?* (ADAAG 4.15.4;4.27.4)

   ✓ Adjust tension on existing controls or modify with easier to use controls.

4. **Does the fountain protrude no more than 4" into the circulation space?** (ADAAG 4.4)

   ✓ Place a cane-detectable barrier on each side at floor level.

5. *Is the flow of the water regulated in a steady stream?*

   ✓ *Adjust the water pressure flow to prevent sudden rushes of water from the spout.*

6. **Is the flow of water at least 4" high, or, if a round bowl, within 3" of the front edge of the fountain?** (ADAAG 4.15.3)

   ✓ Adjust water pressure so flow is high enough to allow a cup under the flow.

Alarms (ADAAG 4.28) **& Emergency Egress** (ADAAG 4.1.3(14),4.28)

1. **Do all alarms have both flashing lights and audible signals?** (ADAAG 4.28; 4.1.3(14))

   ✓ Install visible and audible alarms.

2. **Are emergency exits and evacuation plans well marked and/or publicized?**

   NOTE: Signs with red letters on a white background may be difficult for some older persons to read.

   ✓ Add additional high contrast and large letter exit signs.
   ✓ *Make evacuation plan easily accessible to visitors or permanent residents or employees.*
   ✓ *Identify staff who can provide assistance and who will check the area if facility is evacuated.*

9 Complete Guide to Supplies, Services, and Resources

Overview

9.1   Supplies and Equipment

Keeping facilities clean requires supplies—both expendable ones that will need to be replaced on a regular basis and equipment that is more long-lasting. Equipment intended for heavy-duty use will need to be kept in good repair in order to be functional. It is both cost effective and a time-saver to have these items on hand so they are there when needed.

One of the primary reasons there is a plan for maintenance is that it is important that the library be kept in a clean and safe condition at all times. The main idea behind a housekeeping plan is to remove items that are not part of fixtures, furniture, and carpeting and restore them back to a clean condition.

The process of cleaning surfaces and the frequency of cleaning is dependent upon the type of surface, how much use it gets, and whether some unusual activity has taken place that would increase the need for cleaning. There are specific products and processes that experts tell us are better than others for particular surfaces, and consideration should be given to these. Manufacturers will also recommend particular supplies that should be used to clean their products. Therefore, circumstances may require that a variety of supplies and equipment be in place in order to accomplish the cleaning that needs to be done in an efficient, effective manner.

If your library system is part of a larger municipality or organization, and you have the opportunity to purchase supplies under a consortia arrangement, there is no doubt that you will receive better discounts. You will want to consider if you should purchase supplies that will last for several months, since the more you buy, the greater the discounts. If you are located a great distance from a supplier, buying in bulk may also reduce shipping charges. However, this may not be feasible if storage is a problem.

9.2   Tools and Equipment List

Tools

Work gloves (cloth and disposable plastic)
Flashlights and batteries
Extension cords (a variety of lengths and weights)
Measuring tape (12–foot flexible)
Hammer
Screwdrivers—flat-sided blade and Phillips
Pliers
Drill
Vise grips
Wrench adjustable
Wrench Allen
First-aid kit
Plumber's plunger
Plumber's snake
Shovel (dirt and snow)
Rakes
Feather duster
Cleaning cloths assorted
Cleaning brushes assorted
Sponges
Brooms
Mops dust
Mops wet
Buckets
Trash receptacles
Safety glasses or goggles
Hard hats
Dust masks
Hoses
Safety signs (example: "Wet Floor")

Equipment

Vacuum cleaner
Lawn mower
Edger
Weeder
Leaf blower
Snowblower
Carpet shampooer
Wet vacuum cleaner
Electric hedge clippers
Extension ladders

9.3   Recommended Supplies to Have on Hand

Glass cleaner
Furniture polish
Carpet shampoo
Floor wax
Trash bags
Leaf bags
Soap or detergent
Spot remover or solvent
Graffiti remover
Cleansers or abrasives
Bleach or disinfectant
Paper towels
Bathroom tissue
Liquid soap
Air freshener
Storage cabinet for chemicals
Labels and information sheets for chemicals
Antidotes for chemicals
Salt or sand for ice melting
Washes
Nails, screws, nuts, bolts (have a variety on hand)

9.4   Supply Sources

In addition to the many local sources you have for supplies and equipment, there are national companies that specialize in supplies for maintenance and facilities management. The following is a selected list of some of the more prominent companies. You will want to check with several to get the best prices. It bears repeating that centralized purchasing may have already completed this research for you. Buying in bulk always saves money, but be sure you have adequate storage to house the products. This list is a sampling and we hope it will be of assistance to you. The authors do not specifically recommend or endorse any of these.

A–1 Janitorial Supply and Equipment
1419 Eastway Drive
Charlotte, NC 28205–2205

Abrasive Products, Inc.
P.O. Box 250
Fortville, IN 46040

Americorp International
2309 Airport Road
Waterford, MI 48327

Arrow Star
3–1 Park Plaza
Glen Head, NY 11545

Bobrick Washroom Equipment
11611–T Hart Street
No. Hollywood, CA 91605–5800

Champion America
1333 Highland Road E.
Macedonia, OH 44056–2399

Clean Water Systems International
2322 Marina Drive
Klamath Falls, OR 97601

Consolidated Plastics, Inc.
8181 Darron Road
Twinburg, OH 44087

Doty & Sons
Concrete Products
1275 East Street
Sycamore, IL 60178

Economy Maintenance Supply Company
P.O. Box 349
Fairfax Station, VA 22039

Emed Co., Inc.
P.O. Box 369
Buffalo, NY 14240

Gempler's
P.O. 270
100 Countryside Drive
Belleville, WI
1-800–382–8473

Global Industrial Equipment
22 Harbor Park Drive
Port Washington, NY 11050

Glover Equipment Company
P.O. Box 405
Cockeysville, MD 21030

Government Products News
110 Superior Avenue
Cleveland, OH 44114–2543

Hotsy Cleaning Systems
2428 W. Central Avenue
Missoula, MT 59801–6464

Lewis Supply Company, Inc.
P.O. Box 220
Memphis, TN 38101

Lyons Safety
P.O. Box 9006
Menomonee Falls, WI 53051

Maintenance World
P.O. Box 1333
Pleasantville, NY 08232

Massune First Aid & Safety
490 Fillmore Avenue
Tonawanda, NY 14150

National Fire Prevention Association
1 Batterymarch Park
Quincy, MA 02269–9101

Neutron Industries
7107 N. Black Canyon Highway
Phoenix, AZ 85021–7661

Procter & Gamble Paper Products Company
P.O. Box 599
Cincinnati, OH 45201

PROMACO, Inc.
3714 Runge Street
Franklin Park, IL 60131–1112

Raymond Products Company
951 E. Hennepin Avenue
Minneapolis, MN 55414

Rest Room World
825 Noah's Road
Pleasantville, NJ 08232–6333

Securall
5122 North Street Road #39
La Porte, IN 46350

Sempra Energy Facilities Management
555 W. 5th Street
Los Angeles, CA 90013

Seton
20 Thompson Road
Branford, CT 06405–0819

Signtech, Inc.
4669 Hwy. 90 West
San Antonio, TX 78237

Sweet's Group Product News
2 Penn Plaza
9th Floor
New York, NY 10121

United Receptacle
Pottsville, PA

Upbeat
4350 Duncan Avenue
St. Louis, MO 63110

Vallen Safety Supply Company
240 Center Court
Anchorage, AK 99518

Ward Thompson Paper, Inc.
P.O. Box 3839
Butte, MT 59702

W. R. Meadows, Inc.,
P.O. Box 667
Walnut, CA 91788

Young and Vann Supply Company
P.O. Box 757
Birmingham, AL 35201

Youngs
55 Cherry Lane
Souderton, PA 18964–1550

9.5 Other Services

Because there are special concerns for libraries regarding moisture with collections, we have included a few other resources that might be of help.

Moisture Control Services
79 Monroe Street
Amesbury, MA 01913

Munters
800 I-Can-Dry (800 422–6379)

Sterilizing Services
Cumberland Industrial Park
Cumberland, RI 02862

9.6   Where to Go for Help

While the task of overseeing a facility may be overwhelming at times, there are indeed resources available that can be helpful to you. It is always advisable to check with state, local, and federal agencies that provide publications, video tapes, and even consultant services that will assist you with this task. Our general collections may not contain resources that can help us, but wonderful materials are often produced by insurance companies; they often maintain libraries of professional materials on loss control, safety-related topics, and other building issues.

9.7   Information About Building Regulations

Federal Emergency Management Association (FEMA)
500 C Street SW
Washington, DC 20472

United States Department of Labor
Occupational Safety and Health Administration (OSHA)
(There are regional offices throughout the country. Check *www.osha.gov/*
    for your regional office.)

Environmental Protection Agency (EPA)
(There are regional offices throughout the country. Check *www.epa.gov* for
    information about your area.)

State environmental protection departments

Building Officials and Code Administrators (BOCA)
4051 Flossmoon Road, Country Club Hills, Illinois 60478–5795
708 799–2300
www.bocai.org

Building departments of municipal government

State fire marshals

Local fire marshals

International Facility Management Association
1 E. Greenway Plaza, Suite 1100
Houston, TX 77046
713–623–4362

National Electrical Code

U.S. Public Health Service

State and local health services

Local codes/ordinances

National Institute for Occupational Safety and Health (NIOSH)
944 Chestnut Ridge Road
Morgantown, WV 26505–2888

9.8   Useful Reference Materials

While the materials listed below were not specifically written for library build-ings, quite a bit of the information in them is applicable to our facilities. They are all good sources of additional information.

ADA Accessibility Guidelines for Buildings and Facilities with ADA Technical Assistance Manuals: Checklist for Buildings and Facilities. Carlsbad, CA: Craftsman Book Company, 1998.

Allen, Jeffrey G. *Complying with the ADA.* New York: John Wiley & Sons, 1992.

American Wholesalers and Distributors Directory. 9th edition. New York: Gale, 1997.

Americans with Disabilities Act Handbook. Published in coordination with the U.S. Department of Justice, Civil Rights Division.

———. Americans with Disabilities Act Accessibility Guidelines in The Fed-eral Register, July 26, 1991.

Bannister, Kenneth. *Energy Reduction Through Improved Maintenance.* Woburn, MA: Butterworth-Heinemann, 1999.

———. *Maintenance Management Handbook.* Toronto: Chapman & Hall, 1999.

Biondo, Ronald J. *Introduction to Landscaping: Design, Construction & Main-tenance.* New York: Interstate Printers, 1998.

Blake, William. *Premises Security: A Guide for Security Professionals.* Woburn, MA: Butterworth-Heinemann, 1999.

Boyd, Jon. *Water Problems in Building Exterior Walls: Evaluation and Prevention.* New York: American Society for Testing, 1999.

Brumbaugh, James E. *Roofing and Re-roofing: Installation, Repair and Maintenance.* New York: John Wiley & Sons, 1998.

Cotts, David G. *Facility Management Handbook.* New York: Amacom Book Division, 1998.

———. *Facilities Maintenance & Repair Cost Data 2000.* Kingston, MA: Robert Means, 1999.

Harrison, Maureen, and Steve Gilbert. *The Americans with Disabilities Act Handbook.* Beverly Hills, CA: Excellent Books, 1992.

Herzog, Peter. *Energy-Efficient Operation of Commercial Buildings.* Los Angeles: McGraw-Hill, 1997.

Himmel, Ethel, and William J. Wilson. *Planning for Results: A Public Library Transformation Process.* Chicago: American Library Association, 1998.

Jewell, Don. *Privatization of Public Assembly Facility Management.* New York: Krieger Publishing, 1998.

———. *Library Space Planning Guide.* Hartford, CT: The Connecticut State Library, 2000.

Leighton, Phillip D., and David C. Weber. *Planning Academic and Research Library Buildings.* 3rd edition. Chicago: American Library Association, 1999.

Levitt, Alan. *Disaster Planning and Recovery: A Guide for Facility Professionals.* New York: John Wiley & Sons, 1997.

Lewis, Bernard. *Facility Manager's Operation and Maintenance Handbook,* New York: McGraw-Hill, 1999.

———. *Facility Manager's Portable Handbook.* New York: McGraw-Hill, 1999.

Lushington, Nolan, and Willis N. Mills Jr. *Libraries Designed for Users: A Planning Handbook.* New York: Gaylord Professional Publications, 1979.

Piper, James. *Operations and Maintenance Manual for Energy Management.* New York: M.E. Sharpe, 1999.

Sievert, Richard. *Total Productive Facilities Management: A Comprehensive Program.* Kingston, MA: Robert Means, 1998.

Stoneham, Derek. *Maintenance Management and Technology Handbook.* Englewood Cliffs, NJ: Elsevier, 1998.

Westerkamp, Thomas A. *Maintenance Manager's Standard Manual.* Englewood Cliffs, NJ: Prentice Hall, 1999.

Wulfinghoff, Donald. *Energy Efficiency Manual.* State College, PA: Energy Institute Press, 2000.

9.9 Web Sites

The Internet can be a valuable tool for finding services and support for the facilities manager. The following are among the most prominent of the Web sites that relate to facilities management.

www.energyservices.net

www.facilitiesmanagement.com (supplies, sourcing, and procurement of materials)

www.fema.gov. (Federal Emergency Management Agency)

www.fmdata.com (facility planning and management of data; good site to find experts and consultants)

www.fmlink.com (includes professional development materials)

www.facilitiesnet.com (buyer's guides, product literature)

www.usda.gov/oo/ (technical information, procurement, conservation issues)

Glossary of Facilities Management Terms

As with any industry or profession, there is a vocabulary that goes along with facility management. Even though we all try not to speak in our professional "shorthands," it happens. It is helpful for the library director to become familiar with these terms in order to better communicate with the vendors and contractors who will be involved in some of the processes that will occur at your site.

Abrasive cleaners: Cleaning substances that are composed of a grainy material.

Acoustical tile: Tile made of wood fibers, vegetable fibers, cork, or metal that is used to control sound volume.

Activity areas: Places that are designed to support particular functions. An example would be a small seminar room for a meeting for six to eight people.

Air ducts: Pipes that carry warm or cool air from heating and air conditioning units to other parts of the facility.

Amenity areas: Areas of the building that are used for nonwork activities. They include lounges and vending areas.

Asbestos: Hazardous substance that was formerly used in insulation, floor tiles, and other older building materials.

Audit: This word has several applications. In the financial arena, it means the review of all financial records to ensure that monies were spent in the appropriate fashion. For the facility, it refers to the inspection of the basics of the building's infrastructure or specific systems.

Bearing wall: Wall that supports a floor or the roof of a building

Building core: Interior areas, including elevators, rest rooms, fire stairs, mechanical shafts, and janitorial, electrical, and phone closets.

Building envelope: Total layers forming the building parameter, including the roof, walls, windows, doors, and foundation.

Calibration: Units of measurement on a gauge.

Circuit breaker: Safety device that interrupts electric current when the flow reaches a level that exceeds the system design.

Concurrent maintenance: Ability to shut down and work on a major building system (heat, air conditioning, and so on) during normal business hours without disrupting the facility's operations.

Corrective maintenance: Activities that are performed because of equipment or system failure, restoring the area to a specified level of performance.

Cost of Operation: Total cost associated with the day-to-day operation of a facility. It includes all maintenance and repair; administrative overhead; labor costs; janitorial; housekeeping, and other cleaning costs; utilities; and all costs associated with roadways and grounds.

Cost-effective: Plan where there are periodic reviews to identify areas where there may be cost savings while still maintaining quality.

Cyclical maintenance: Maintenance that is predictable and it is performed on a regular basis.

Deferred maintenance: Unaccomplished maintenance tasks due to situations due to shortages of funds or personnel or other specific causes.

Degree-day: Unit of measurement that is equal to the number of degrees that the mean temperature for a 24–hour period varies from a base temperature of 65 degrees.

Detergent: Water-soluble synthetic cleaning agent.

Disinfectant: Cleaning agent that destroys bacteria.

End-to-end reliability: Backing up all areas and systems that could potentially fail, so the facility can operate with no downtime.

Ergonomic equipment: Equipment designed to reduce operator fatigue and discomfort.

Facility Management: Practice of coordinating the physical workplace with the people and the work of the organization. According to the International Facilities Management Association, this practice should incorporate the principles of business administration, architecture, and behavioral and engineering sciences.

Fault tolerance: Ability of the facility to respond to a failure such as a chiller breakdown or a power interruption without losing productivity or affecting temperature-sensitive equipment.

Fire corridors: Designated escape routes to be used in case of a fire.

Flashing: Metal that is used around angles and junctions in roofs and exterior walls to prevent leaks.

Footprint: Working square footage that is required to support a particular function. This includes space that is used for furniture as well as for chair movement and traffic circulation.

Foundation: Masonry or concrete below ground level upon which a structure is built.

Glazing: Fitting glass into windows and doors.

Grout: Mortar that is used to fill in spaces and cracks in walls, tiles, and so forth.

HVAC: Acronym that is commonly used to describe heating, ventilation, and air-conditioning systems.

Insourcing: Process of bringing in outside consultants to measure the operation against a standard benchmark and make recommendations for improvements. The internal staff then takes the recommendations and refers them to the appropriate individuals for action.

Layout: Plan created by a space planner, interior designer, or architect, showing the utilization of space.

Material Safety Data Sheet (MSDS): Product information for chemicals, including cleaning agents, that provides data on safe storage, fire prevention, handling, and mixing instructions, as well as first-aid treatment.

Mechanical area: That portion of the building designated to house mechanical equipment and utility services.

Outsourcing: Full or partial transfer of facilities management functions to an outside firm. The library manages the outsourcing contract rather than the entire facilities management function.

Payback period: Length of time it takes for an initial investment to be recovered.

Phasing: Scheduling the conversion or repair of a critical facility system so that downtime is eliminated or at least minimized.

Pitch: Angle of the slope of the roof.

Points of failure: Areas that could fail and cause disruption in critical operations.

Preventive maintenance: Planned actions undertaken to retain an item at a specified level of performance by providing repetitive, scheduled repairs. These prolong the system operation and useful life and include such tasks as inspection, cleaning, lubrication, and part replacement.

Punch list: List of deficiencies or incomplete or unacceptable work that is compiled by the project manager during the final inspection of a project.

Redundancy: Building duplicate critical systems into the facility, such as dual telecommunications from different carriers, to ensure continuous, uninterrupted operations.

Relative humidity: Quantity of water vapor that is in the air at a specific temperature compared to the maximum amount of water the air can hold at that temperature. Usually this is expressed in percentages and is an important reading due to the nature of the materials that are held within libraries.

Retrofit: Addition of new materials or equipment or the redesign of an area within a building that changes it from its original construction. An example would be the retrofitting of rest rooms for ADA accommodations.

Risk management: Process of making and carrying through decisions that reduce or minimize the adverse effects of accidental loss upon an organization. It must be able to adjust to changing organizational requirements.

Sick building: Building wherein heating, ventilation, and air-conditioning systems have become contaminated with harmful microbes.

Sole-source procurement: Procurement awarded to a single vendor without competition.

Support areas: Mail centers, copy centers, conference rooms, storage areas, security areas, shipping and receiving areas.

Survivability level: Ability of a facility to withstand a major disaster, such as a hurricane, earthquake, or bombing.

Valve: Device that controls the flow of a fluid.

Workplace standards: Guidelines used to allocate workspace on a system-wide basis according to a set of criteria that, in a library, is usually based on work function. In the corporate world, workspace may be assigned according to position, title, or seniority.

Workstations: Any space at which a function is accomplished. It may be enclosed or open space.

Index

About the Authors

MARCIA TROTTA is the director of the Meriden Public Library in Connecticut and a past president of the Connecticut Library Association. She was chosen Outstanding Librarian by the Connecticut Library Association in 1986 and again in 1993. In 2001 she was awarded the Faith Hecktoen Award by the Connecticut Library Association. Marcia is Adjunct Professor at the School of Library Science and Information Technology at Southern Connecticut State University.

CARMINE TROTTA is the director of Support Systems for Boys Village in Milford, Connecticut. He has been the chair of the White House Conference on Library and Information Services Task Force since 1996.